Out of My Heart

BOOKS BY
AGNES SLIGH TURNBULL

NOVELS

The Rolling Years
Remember the End
The Day Must Dawn
The Bishop's Mantle
The Gown of Glory
The Golden Journey

FOR CHILDREN

Jed, the Shepherd's Dog
Elijah the Fish-bite

NONFICTION

Out of My Heart

Out of
My Heart

by

Agnes Sligh Turnbull

HOUGHTON MIFFLIN COMPANY BOSTON

The Riverside Press Cambridge

SECOND PRINTING

For
Pat and Paul O'Hearn

Preface

THE DESIRE to write their memoirs seems to occur to many men and women as they grow older. Those especially who have long been more or less articulate as writers often feel a certain compulsion to narrate their own life's adventures for a change. The urge which has fallen upon me, however, is slightly different. My life has been quiet and to a large extent uneventful. Even if it had been excitingly colorful I fear that a long strain of Scotch-Irish blood would have inhibited me from laying bare the secrets of the years. The question that has kept recurring to me is, have all these years I have now lived taught me anything of value? Like many other human beings I have known great happiness and great sorrow, a fair measure of success and perhaps an equal measure of disappointments. Is there from all this living a certain residuum of experience which, if not actually wisdom, may have some possible significance when passed on to others? I am not at all sure; but I have decided to set down a few of the most important lessons life has presented to me. I do not mean that I, myself, have mastered them. Far from it. I do mean that if I could live my time over, these are the ones I would try most earnestly to practice.

As I have indicated, there is no attempt at autobiography in this book, but there are constant background references to my childhood, because in any life the early years are basic and evocative.

A. S. T.

Maplewood
New Jersey

Contents

I
The Great Incentive

"The spirit of man is the candle of the Lord."

WHEN I WAS GROWING UP in a small village in western Pennsylvania there lived across the street from us three elderly maiden ladies. Their house was a sort of cottage with a small apple orchard on one side, and a wide spreading pine tree at the garden edge, shading it upon the other. An iron fence bounded the lot, the gate opening upon two walks that diverged in a V, one leading to the front of the house, and one around the pine tree to the lattice-screened porch at the back. The unusual feature of these walks was that their gravel width was edged with white shells. As I recall it all now, I am mystified as to where these could have come from, for we were far from the sea, and vacation journeys to it were as much unthought of in the town in those days as trips to the moon. The presence of the alien shells, however, always gave me a thrill as hinting of far-off beauty and mysterious delights.

The oldest sister, Miss Margaret, was tall, poised, and noble in character and countenance. Once, after a meeting of the Women's Missionary Society, a five-dollar bill was found in the collection basket. A secret discussion ensued. It was decided that only one person would have made such a sacrificial offering, for money was scarce in our village. When asked, Miss Margaret confessed with embarrassment that her brother in the city had sent her the bill that she might buy herself a new bonnet, but since she didn't need such a thing she preferred to give the money to foreign missions.

Miss Sallie, the second sister, was handsome, fluttery and fussy in her manner, with an elaborate white pompadour and puffs, lace-edged ruffles and gold bracelets. She was given to original aphorisms which were spoken airily without reference to any conversational content. Her favorite, I remember, was: "'Tis better farther on, you know! Better farther on."

The youngest sister, Miss Beckie, the smallest and least good-looking of the three, was animated by a great purpose in life. She had A Cause to which she was devoted. This was Temperance. It was she who shepherded us children into an organization called The Loyal Temperance Legion, where we learned about Neal Dow and Frances E. Willard, and sang such rousing songs as

> When asked to drink
> We'll smile and turn
> Our glasses *upside down!*

She also made an annual visit to the school. The teacher, a really brilliant man who luckily for us was rusticating in our small community, always received her with respect and, as it

were, gave her the floor. With her little black bonnet bob-
bing in her enthusiasm, and her bow of white ribbon showing
conspicuously on her coat lapel, she proceeded then to tell us
of the terrors of King Alcohol. We were asked to turn to
page sixty in our old Blaisdell's *Physiologys* where a drunkard's liver was pictured to our horrified view! At the end of
her discourse came a few remarks upon cigarettes — "coffin
nails," as she called them. These concluding words were addressed, of course, to the boys alone. The idea that any
young girl would ever smoke was, like the realization of the
airplane and the atom bomb, reserved for a much later day.

As Miss Beckie poured out upon the young males (who
had doubtless already experimented freely with the forbidden
weed in the back alleys) all the ghastly dangers to body, mind
and soul of the use of cigarettes, the boys listened politely,
but rolled an eye now and then or coughed with feigned
nonchalance behind their warty hands.

We girls, however, drank it all in with unquestioning interest, the horror of the drunkard's liver and the "coffin nails"
bringing a delightful diversion in the tedium of the school
day.

When it seemed as though the three sisters would live on
forever in their quaint house, Miss Margaret fell and, after a
long, patient illness, died. I remember the morning I went
over, as the custom of our village was, to "see" her. I went
along the shell-bordered walk to the back door. Miss Sallie
and Miss Beckie sat together silently in the kitchen where the
coal range was polished to shining and the magnificent old
"dresser" added an elegance of which I'm sure both the sisters
and I were then unaware. I went up the stairs alone to the

room where Miss Margaret lay. There was nothing but peace in that chamber. It was a June morning and in the apple orchard outside the robins were singing. A soft breeze moved the curtains. I looked upon Miss Margaret's noble face and felt for the first time the dignity of death.

It was after this that something happened to Miss Beckie. The brightness of her spirit became gradually dimmed. The eager enthusiasm, the quick-eyed efficiency ceased. She went no more to visit the school nor to lead the Loyal Temperance Legion. She sat at home in a dark brooding melancholy from which she never recovered. She felt, in the hard Calvinistic phraseology to which she was accustomed, that she was "lost"; that she had somehow committed "the unpardonable sin"; that she was doomed to utter perdition.

The tragedy of Miss Beckie struck deeply into my youthful consciousness. That her cheerful, useful, innocent life should end in this darkness posed a problem I could not answer; but it has pursued me over the years until I have come at last to wonder whether there has not been one mistake at least made by most of us in our attitude toward God. While Miss Beckie's case was an extreme one, there are all too many variations of it now in our own day, ranging from the common feelings of futility and frustration to those of actual melancholy. This alarming growth of mental depression has touched the young as well as the old.

While most of these feelings may have their root in physical disorders, it is still true that if the spirit is soundly integrated it will not so likely be affected by assaults upon the body. This word "integration" is tossed about rather freely these days, but the definition I like best is found in Herbert

Spencer's own use of it: *the process by which the manifold is compacted into the relatively simple and permanent.* In other words, then, if a man or a woman has succeeded either consciously or unconsciously in coming to simple and permanent terms with life (and the universe in general), there is little danger of emotional disturbances. And this simple and permanent acceptance of life, this tranquillity at the core of personality, is most likely, psychologists tell us, to be the result of an inner sense of *worth*.

Of course, theologically speaking, the spell of the old Puritan and the Calvinist is still over us all. According to them, men were worms of the earth, fit for nothing in themselves but "the blackness of darkness forever." This hard religious attitude was, of course, the cause of poor little Miss Beckie's tragedy. While many people now either do not know or do not care about these harsh tenets of an earlier faith, the atmosphere of their thinking may still be unconsciously colored by them.

There are many other contributing factors which cause a lack of the sense of personal worth. The new scientific and mechanistic triumphs certainly are among these. The pioneers, and the farmers of a past day who plowed their fields, sowed their grain and reaped the harvest with their own hands, were likely to have a greater inner satisfaction than the million cogs in the million modern wheels can possibly have. And I very much suspect that the women of the old days, too, may have set more value upon themselves as they spun their yarn and baked their bread than we do in our laborsaving, push-button era.

In a remarkable little book called *Letters of the Scattered*

Brotherhood, there is cited still another cause, a general one, for the depression that overtakes men and women.

It may help you to remember once in a while [the author says] how deeply the human being is enmeshed in the flesh, and what is not often thought of, the flesh is very old. Although it is consciously renewed in an almost incredibly short time, a few months, the cells have the stamp of race memories and experiences of the ages past and that is why this tired flesh, the body of the human race, which has met savagery, war, sorrow and grief, is so friendly to despair.

But no matter what the reason, there is in our own time widespread tension, unease and restlessness with generally depressive emotions. Even the most stable of us certainly have frequent feelings of inadequacy and futility when the old classic cry of *Cui bono?* is translated freely into "Oh, what's the use?"

One day in my reading I came across a beautiful and startling line. It occurs in the poetic works of Solomon, once King of Israel. This is it:

The spirit of man is the candle of the Lord.

I took this at once at its face value without reading farther. No matter what the great wise man had in his mind, here was a thought for which I had been waiting, and which suggested a new slant to all my thinking. Suppose that man's spirit could actually afford *light* to God himself! This, of course, was in direct contradiction to that really dreadful answer in the old Westminster Shorter Catechism which I committed to memory (quite happily, I might add) as a child.

"All mankind by their fall lost communion with God, are

under his wrath and curse and so made liable to all the miseries of this life, to death itself and to the pains of hell forever."

I hope the divines who once wrote that have now learned better!

I began to think in earnest about man in his relation to the universe. When we consider the incredible number of stars in the vasty deeps of the sky — a number which confounds the imagination of even the greatest astronomer — it does seem illogical to suppose that only upon one tiny speck called Earth are there creatures of intelligence and understanding. If this *is* so, then man must be God's last and great experiment and so of major importance to Him.

It seems more reasonable, however, to assume that there is perhaps an infinitude of stars and other planets upon which there is life revolving around other suns. Development there in some cases might conceivably have taken place along parallel lines with that of earth; but it is highly improbable that because of this it has produced the same results. No, we must conclude, I think, that the race of men, as we know it, is unique in all the universe and therefore must have a peculiar value to God himself. According to the old writer, He actually depends upon us for *light*.

Soon after this line began to haunt me I happened one day to be talking to a priest, on the beach, of all places. During our chat I brought forth my new treasure and the idea it held for me. He reacted to it almost violently.

"No," he said, "God needs nothing from us! *Nothing!*"

But, as I thought this over afterwards, I wondered how anyone could accept the concept of God as a father and deny

that he has any need of us. Was there ever an earthly father
interested only in *giving* to his children? Let us say this act is
a primary necessity because of the child's weakness and in-
sufficiency compared to his strength and opportunity. But
having given to the child he is then eager to receive from him
love, gratitude and, most of all, perhaps, happiness. It is the
joy of our children that lights our hearts as parents; it is their
little triumphs that mean more to us than our larger ones; it
is their blundering efforts to be good and their penitent tears
that bring peace to a father's mind.

The sad parents of the world are those who give and give
and give sacrificially and receive back no spoken words of
thanks, of love, of solicitous devotion; who see no happy
growth because of their constant care. Their hearts are indeed unlighted.

When this is all true of a natural father it seems to me very
wrong to assume that God, whom we have been taught on
the highest authority to call our Heavenly Father, has no
need of us; that his whole function is to give, to bestow; that
he craves nothing from us but the worship which is offered
half in fear and half in awe.

There is a striking line in the old *Theologia Germanica* of
1497: *I would fain be to the Eternal Goodness, what his own
hand is to a man.*

And so we return again to Solomon's beautiful imagery,
which I had interpreted in my own way.

The spirit of man is the candle of the Lord.

I thought of Solomon's father, King David, who has always been such a comfort to me. Not only is he my favorite

poet, but he inspires me in all my dreadful failures. He was guilty of murder. He was guilty of adultery. He knew excruciating sorrow. He was crushed by a remorse so black that he was submerged by it. Yet up from the depths of all this, like a lark in spring, rose his spirit in love, in thanksgiving, in praise, always praise, to the very gate of heaven. I don't think we can possibly miss or minimize the significance of this.

Suppose that the brave, bright upleap of our own hearts was of actual *help* to God. Suppose, as William James suggests, that our triumphs over pain, sin, sorrow and remorse give him "increase of very being." What then?

If we truly believed that the glow of our spirits lighted up the heart of the Eternal even as a candle is lighted, it would surely increase our sense of individual worth and make our hearts more resilient to bear the burdens of life. It would, indeed, furnish the Great Incentive, not only to courage and goodness, but to something perhaps as important to God — our own happiness.

II
The Mystery of the Obvious

"What is that in thine hand?"

MY MOTHER'S DEAREST FRIEND was Miss Sarah. They had been girls together and a strong affection bound them all through the years. Miss Sarah was tall and spare with thin patrician features, wise, kindly eyes and a slow but beautiful smile. She lived "over the creek" in a large brick house and could reach the long sloping street of the village only by crossing the covered wooden bridge which spanned the Loyalhanna. She liked to walk and so, basket on arm, often covered the mile between the houses and came to call on my mother. Then I listened in pleased surprise as their nicknames *Sallie* and *Cinnie* were tossed back and forth between them. Miss Sarah frequently brought me little presents: a bottle of perfume, a handkerchief, a copy of the musical magazine *Etude* for a Valentine, and once a motto from Whittier for my bedroom wall. I still remember a few of the lines:

> And so I find it well to come
> For deeper rest to this still room;
> For here the habit of the soul
> Feels less the outer world's control.

She was the sort of person who would select that gift for a young girl. One day when she came she brought in her basket a small booklet with an arresting title. I read the words over later with curiosity. *What Is That in Thine Hand?* I had been brought up on the Bible so I soon placed them as the question God asked Moses before he answered, "A rod." According to the old narrative it became much more than a mere shepherd's stick before he was through with it. I read the little book now intently. The purport of it was that each human being held something mysterious and valuable *in his hand*, which if recognized and if blessed by God could develop into a means of power. The thing held, whether talent, skill, quality or opportunity, might be so obvious or so humble as to be entirely overlooked (even as the crook seemed an ordinary enough attribute to Moses as he looked after his father-in-law's sheep) but which still possessed enormous possibility.

The little essay emphasized the fact that we are likely to be mentally blind to what is close and familiar. As I recall, it was addressed particularly to the humble, everyday men and women who do not feel their lives are of any great value in the eternal scheme. With great tenderness the writer begged them to look closely at themselves to see if perhaps there was not "some thing in their hands" of which they had not been aware.

I read this over and over. The striking theme with its

beautiful clothing of language (whose author I cannot remember) made a deep impression upon me and has kept recurring to me over the years. I feel it is unfortunate in my
own case that only recently the query has hit me with full
force. My thinking of it now has been along two lines, and
the results are so simple and unoriginal that I hesitate to set
them down. Yet, I feel impelled to do so.

Through these present times of overwhelming danger and
crisis when the world seems to topple, right itself and then
tremble again; when we live, as it were, with the sword of
Damocles poised above us, while great emergencies threaten,
subside and recur, there exists a strange situation for the
average citizen. I am a persistent optimist. I still believe in
the ultimate triumph of peace; but this does not alter the fact
that along the way I shudder at the exigencies which are filled
with jeopardy.

Now the thought which has so often overtaken me is that
across the world the whole race of mankind want to *live* and
go about their normal affairs; they want the world to stay
steady without war or cataclysm. And yet, even with their
preponderance of numbers, they are helpless. The decisions
for life or death, for continuance or annihilation are in the
hands of a relatively few men scattered over the globe.

To bring it down to our own nation, we are a free people.
We elect the leaders who will bear the responsibilities of government. But no matter how good and wise and dedicated
they are, the fact is they are also human and fallible; and the
further fact is that all the millions of the rest of us are power-
less, impotent to affect our own fate or to stave off ultimate
disaster.

As I read the morning paper or listen to the news analysts I often recall the beautiful state of ignorance in which we all lived when I was a child. The small, peaceful village bounded our horizon. The only times we were faced with facts about foreign countries was when an occasional "returned missionary" presented stereopticon views at church showing people of Africa or China or India. Even then we accepted this in a sense as entertainment where diversions were few, gave our modest offerings to the cause, and came home with minds undisturbed.

The village men, such as my father, might sit in the winter evenings around the stove in the general store and exchange profound and completely unknowing views as to whether one day there might be trouble with "Rooshia" or Japan. But here among the cracker barrels the question was purely academic, so to speak, and the men, upon leaving, walked peacefully home under the stars, shedding international suppositions as easily as their winter overcoats. Now, we are torn constantly by the dangers of a world grown small which presses closely in upon us.

As I was considering recently the fact of the powerlessness of the millions of everyday people to work their will upon events, I was struck suddenly by this old question, "What is that in thine hand?" And as I thought of it, as in a lightning flash, it occurred to me that we all do hold one thing and *only* one thing as a weapon for good. This is prayer.

Now the most striking fact about prayer is that it represents the one point where people of every religion under the sun meet. They all pray. The exercise, even if used only in time of extremity, is instinctive and universal. In the realm

of what we may call "thinking" people, there are two opinions held regarding it. The great majority believe, consciously or unconsciously, that the prayer of the human spirit
reaches the heart of God himself and receives some kind of
answer from him; another group feels that prayer is merely
a psychic reaction which generates effects in its own realm.

The thought that struck me so violently was that if there
should be a concerted effort of prayer for the men who are
laboring for peace and for those who are obstructing it; if
with intensity and directness the free peoples — all the house-
wives, the professional men, the truck drivers, the creative
artists and the laborers — all of them should once a day,
wherever they were, lift their hearts in dynamic appeal that
their own leaders might have wisdom and guidance, and
that those personalities behind the Iron Curtain who have
brought fear upon us all might be changed in their minds,
might see the danger and themselves recoil from it — if this
were done there would surely be released such an explosive
force across the world as would produce effects.

Such a simple but powerful weapon we each hold in our
hands! I don't know how a great crusade of prayer could be
started, but if it could be done I believe absolutely in its results. The times in which we are now living are not suitable
ones in which to deny or discredit the possibility of mysterious power; not as long as we calmly accept radar, radio and
television. They all employ forces beyond our comprehen-
sion. Why should we doubt then that the vehement outward
and upward reach of our minds and souls would occasion a
release of some mighty energy, some compelling potency
from God himself, in answer to our call? Meanwhile, we

might remember that once long ago a categorical statement was made about the efficacy of the prayer of only two or three. I, for one, am trying steadily to follow this practice.

The other way in which the question "What is that in thine hand?" suddenly struck me with such force was its application to human relationships, especially those of the family. Here it is so very easy to be affected by the familiarity which, if it does not "breed contempt," does often breed a kind of emotional blindness.

For example, in most marriages the early years are blessed with children. There is always at first the overwhelming pride and satisfaction of the young parents. But as the number of these blessings multiplies perhaps faster than the family income, there are likely to be times when the patience of both father and mother becomes strained. The former may come home from his job with taut nerves and all the anxieties of the breadwinner to find bedlam and strident cries, while the mother who has been trying all day to deal with three or four different and restless little personalities, along with the doing of the housework, may be tired to the point of exhaustion. I remember well the wail of an ailing young woman who once said to me, "It's the children! That's what's the matter with me. If I could only get away for a little while from *the children!*"

Probably many young mothers have either expressed the same sentiment or thought it, at times. But there is no real cure for this situation in the sense of altering it. The change must be in the parent. Nature goes about her business with a calm and eternal wisdom, and we must all accept it. Young children, no matter how ardently longed for, how tenderly beloved, are likely to be shrill and noisy and at times, in their small way, obdurate. They bring into the home joy unspeakable, but they also bring a certain confusion and much work. The thing, however, that older people like myself come to realize is that these "little years" are not only infinitely precious, but that the swiftness of their passing is exceeded only by their importance. For the thing which young parents hold in their hand is childhood itself, that strange and beautiful and evanescent land; that mysterious golden country; that realm of faëry. They hold in their hands those magic springs from which their children should forever after draw deep draughts of strength and happy security.

I know that many young mothers feel a certain sense of frustration during their children's early years. As one girl put it, "Is all my college career and my *magna cum* to end in training babies to go to the toilet and eat with a spoon?" Dear young things, I wish I could raise my voice so you would all hear. You are doing the most important work in the world. It has always been so. It always will be. Concentrate during these "little years" upon your children. Play with them, read to them, sing to them, *enjoy* them. There will be plenty of time later on for you to write or paint or head committees, run women's clubs, or serve Great Causes.

I remember reading a poem years ago which still remains with me. (Once again I am ashamed to say I've forgotten the author's name. However, I'm sure plenty of people have forgotten mine so maybe that makes it even!) The first verse ran like this:

> Oh, to come home once more
> When the early dusk is falling,

> To see the nursery windows lighted
> And the children's table spread;
> And "Mother, Mother, Mother,"
> The high child voices calling,
> "The baby was so sleepy that he had to go to bed."

Our home, like most average American ones, did not have a nursery as such, but the essence of the words belongs to us all. I repeat this verse over and over wistfully to myself every autumn, especially "When the early dusk is falling," for there is no music so sweet to a woman's ears as the little eager cry of "Mother, Mother, Mother." And so soon it changes to a more restrained, even though loving welcome.

There is another period when I believe parents are apt to miss the full significance of what they "hold in their hands"; this is when their boys and girls are in the twelve-to-twenty age. We were very lucky during this time with our own daughter. I think we enjoyed every minute of her teens in spite of the hours I lay awake listening for the click of the front door latch which meant that the "date" had brought her safely home and had finally departed. Even admitting the inevitable small anxieties, the three of us — her father, she and I — had such pleasure together during those years, such fun, such closeness! I feel they were the happiest of my life.

But in many cases young girls grow up with all sorts of disturbing emotional fits and starts; young boys are likely to be withdrawn, incomprehensible, even sullen upon occasion, or else wildly erratic. There are again nature's own reasons for all this, but sometimes parents, when their patience is sorely tried, grow not only anxious, but, most dangerous of all, overcritical. They forget the tremendous potential of these plastic years in which a whole lifetime can be affected by harshness, or a lack of sympathetic understanding and guidance.

In his poem called "Germinal," George William Russell (AE) speaks with a terrifying warning of the importance of youth.

> In ancient shadows and twilights
> Where childhood had strayed,
> The world's great sorrows were born
> And its heroes were made.
> *In the lost boyhood of Judas*
> *Christ was betrayed.*

One other reason for looking so carefully at what is in one's hand during our young people's teen years is that they are gone before we know it, leaving a great change behind them. For after this period come college, distant work and wedding days. It is all as every normal parent of us would wish it to be; it is the fulfillment toward which all our hopes, our training, our plans have lead. We watch with satisfaction our children's expanding lives, we welcome and adore the grandchildren when they come; but that close and peculiar joy when our own children sleep under our own roof is gone and nothing can replace it. Each generation learns this by experience and must accept it. On the happy wedding days it is *youth* that has gone and left us lonely, their youth and our own. There comes then the first far intimation that summer does not last forever and that winter looms in the distance. Some day in the future our well-beloved children will experience this, even as our own fathers and mothers before us once did. It is the law of life's changing seasons.

So I would say to the parents of teen-agers, "Look, look at

what you hold in your hand!" It is so precious, so inestimably important, so soon gone. Give your adolescents your best guidance, but most of all, give them the fullness of your love. Laugh with them, be tender to them. *Enjoy them.*

Then of course there is the most intimate of all human relationships, that of husband and wife; here, perhaps more than in any other, partly because of its very intimacy, partly because of the normally longer span of its continuance, there may develop a certain blindness of the heart. The lovers' first ecstatic recognition of each other may grow dim. The husband may come gradually to see only a housekeeper; the wife, a wage earner. Years of familiarity may have covered the fine qualities of each with a sort of film. During late middle age, especially, when the husband has grown a trifle stout and thin of hair, when the wife is graying, has new lines in her face, and has lost her own slimness, there may develop a deadly casualness which can lead to irritability, criticism, and even definite discontent.

This is the time to look at what, in the great majority of cases, lies below the surface: the steady love, the loyalty, the patient sacrifice. This is the time to say, What if I should suddenly lose what I now hold in my hand? Ah, what then, indeed? How the small faults and inadequacies would then sink into relative insignificance! How the great, enduring qualities would shine out when it is tragically too late to praise them. Look, look at what you hold in your hand *now*, before it slips from you.

A marriage may be actually broken in two ways: by death and by divorce. In connection with the latter I remember a story I once read of a foolish woman. She was married to a kindly if rather prosaic man. He had a friend, a debonair, foot-loose bachelor, who came often to their home, enjoying its charm and comfort while bewailing, with apparent sincerity, his own lonely way of life. He showed great admiration for the pretty woman and, within the bounds of decorum, made her feel that he found her desirable and envied his friend's good fortune in having her for his wife. She became convinced finally that she and the bachelor were in love and that she was being wasted as the wife of an uninteresting man when a new and exciting life beckoned her. The first move, she felt, was hers; so when the bachelor, who was a mining engineer, left for an eighteen-months job in the heart of South America, she suddenly asked her husband for a divorce. The poor man was utterly confounded. He tried every persuasion in vain. The wife was then riding on an exhilarating emotional wave. Loved by two men, she was making a dramatic choice between them and was relishing intensely the whole situation. At last the husband provided comfortably for her and sadly saw her off for Reno.

The woman decided after her divorce to travel and visit for some months in the West, timing her return to that of the bachelor, when she would spring the great surprise upon him. It worked out perfectly. From a hotel room in New York she called his apartment. He had just gotten in, and would gladly come over at once. His greeting when he saw her was rather unrestrained since they were alone. She told him then her great piece of news. At once she saw a strange wariness creep over his features. He drew back instinctively. When she emphasized that she was now free and that no obstacle stood in the way of their happiness he became quite eloquent in his unselfish wish for her own welfare. This, he said, could never be with him. He simply *couldn't* ask her to share his unsettled way of life, and so forth, and so forth. He left as soon as possible, looking stunned, but with the vague promise that of course they must see each other again soon.

The woman at last understood. She sat in the coldly impersonal hotel room and saw it all clearly. She knew that she had been a vain and selfish fool. All she craved now was the safety of her former husband's arms. They could be remarried! She would make it all up to him! She called him at his office in a voice that trembled. He was surprised to hear her, inquired kindly how she was and then listened in a dead silence while she poured out her contrition and her wish to come back to him. There was still silence when she finished. Then with real sympathy he said, "I'm sorry but I can do nothing. You see I remarried a month ago. And we are very happy."

This tragic little story may be in itself unique, but it has a universal significance for husbands and wives. Vanity, selfishness, boredom and an inability to hold love by a creative awareness are probably responsible for breaking up more marriages than adultery and other heinous sins. In this most delicate of all relationships there is the necessity for looking intently not only upon what is given us from without, but upon what we may give from within. A man may possess romantic attributes which he has quite forgotten until he searches diligently for their renewal; a woman may have deep springs of charm and appeal which the years have covered over. But these are the leaven that lift a marriage from mediocrity to a glowing affinity of the spirit.

Perhaps the heart of this old and arresting question, *What is that in thine hand?* is the urgent request of us to recognize the joys we hold before, for one reason or another, they are removed from us. Dear old George Herbert, as always, has something pertinent and beautiful to say on this:

> Who would have thought a joy so coy?
> To be offended so,
> And go
> So suddenly away?
> Hereafter I had need
> Take heed,
> Joys among other things
> Have wings
> And watch their opportunities of flight,
> Converting in a moment day to night.

I believe that in each stage of our lives and in every condition we still have in our possession vastly precious gifts which we have only to regard with intelligence in order to appreciate and use as we were doubtless intended to do. We may not, as Moses did with his rod, transfix a king and lead an enslaved people to freedom; though there are men living now in our own time who, by carefully studying their abilities and harnessing them to God's resources, may do just that.

For the rest of us ordinary people, however, it may be enough that we see in our own hands the beauty, the mystery, the power which so often lies hidden in the obvious, and through this new insight live out our lives in usefulness, contentment, and in peace.

III

The Triumph of
Acceptance

"It is hard for thee to kick against the pricks."

ONE OF THE MOST interesting phenomena of contemporary life is the constant discovery that what seems a new or even semimodern idea turns out to be as old as the hills. When we hear the statement that "of the making of many books there is no end," it is surprising to know it is not the wail of a weary present-day critic but the cry of that great man of wisdom, Solomon. "A man's attire, excessive laughter, and gait shew what he is" might very well be Pepys but it happens to be Ecclesiasticus, as is the advice, "Be in peace with many; nevertheless have but one counsellor of a thousand," which one could almost swear came from the lips of Polonius. The whole new approach to psychosomatic diagnosis could be summed up in the very ancient admonition: "Give not over thy mind to heaviness and afflict not thyself in thine own counsel. The gladness of the heart is the life of man, and the joyfulness of a man prolongeth his days."

So in modern psychiatry, when we hear emphasis laid upon the necessity of acceptance as a means to mental health, we remember an expression which shows how very, very old this idea is. The sentence is: "It is hard for thee to kick against the pricks."

This has always conjured up for me a rather touching picture of oxen. I had as I was growing up a pleasant familiarity with horses and to some extent with cows, but I never saw an ox. However, I have a fairly vivid impression of what a yoke of oxen must be like. They are pathetic in a way. Emasculated beasts of burden, with none of the spirited pleasures of the bull, nor yet the peaceful fulfillments of the cow, they pursue their weary, heavy and usually patient course. But once in a while an ox, like a man, resents the lot he cannot change. He becomes restless and irritable, convinced he should be a gay, carefree bull charging in uninhibited fashion over the fields instead of trudging along with his load — and then, he *kicks!*

Now, the ancient farmer had a way of meeting this revolutionary tendency of the ox. He had a row of sharply pointed spikes or "pricks" ranged along the front of the plow or cart, so that when an ox kicked he not only did not free himself from the burden, but received a sore hind leg as well. I still pity the oxen, and I have come to feel that the statement about kicking against the pricks has a definite applicability to our daily lives.

Some comfort may be derived from the fact that no life is completely happy and free from care and anxiety. The whole human race is subject to varying forms of distress. Life is a generous giver of good, but even in childhood we have to learn that the bitter often mingles with the sweet. As the years advance there may come cruel sorrows and situations that tear the heart. I have never been of those who say at such times, *It is God's will.* It seems to me quite wrong to blame the ills of the world upon God. I am reminded of the story I heard of a New England farmer who ate a whole mince pie on top of a huge dinner of pork and beans and died that night of acute indigestion. At the funeral the minister spoke feelingly of its being the *will of God* that this man should die and that all should accept the tragedy in that spirit. This seems to me a cowardly shifting of the blame. It would surely have been the will of God for the man to live out a normal useful, happy life. It was the farmer himself who broke the laws of health and had to pay accordingly.

But aside from an extreme case such as this, there are countless ones in which men and women, trying conscientiously and intelligently to do their best, yet suffer from blows that fell them. Disease, disappointment and grief in grave or in minor form beset us all and our big problem is what to do about them. How, as we say to our own hearts, can we bear them?

It is possible that in our present day of material comforts we may expect more of life than our forbears did. We are perhaps a little inclined, as Robert Louis Stevenson put it, "to grasp Fate by the beard and demand joy as a birth-right." The older generations brought up upon the thesis that "we must expect some danger nigh, when most we feel delight," and also upon the McGuffey readers, which if they set a cultural standard also freely dispensed a morbid religious outlook — these older generations, I say, were conditioned by their training and the physical discomforts of their everyday lives to expect trouble and sorrow and cope with it.

I often think of my own grandmother who died when I was a little girl. Her life was certainly not easy. She married a man, by nature a student, who intended to become a minister but who, due to circumstances, had to take over the family farm. He was always a student and never a good farmer so money was scarce. She bore ten children, three of whom died when young. Oh, the unutterable poignancy of those many little graves in the old churchyards! I have noted them with a terrible ache in my heart as I have wandered among the darkening stones. One, I recall, had a small carved lamb asleep upon the diminutive memorial. But most touching of all are the children's age records, two of which I once copied down:

Tommie
Son of J. and M. Smith
Aged 4 years, 2 mos. and 2 days

and

Little Carrie
Aged 1 year, 5 mos. and 16 days.

It is as though the sad parents tried to lengthen out to the last extent the tiny span of living. It would be the mother, I suspect, who with anguished eyes would do the reckoning from the calendar of her heart.

But who in considering the great numbers of these little graves in the past would dare to say that they represented *God's will?* Surely His will is more truly shown in the long, patient sacrificial study of scientists and doctors, the results of which make the death of a little child of rare occurrence now.

However, this most excruciating sorrow had to be borne by the parents of past generations. And that brings me back to my own grandmother. She lived in a substantial brick house, it is true, but one devoid of every single convenience we now deem necessary. Yet I can remember her when she was nearly ninety, her wrinkled face under her white cap, calm, strong and wise. She, I'm sure, had learned from the years not to kick against the pricks.

In bygone days the word which was greatly emphasized in connection with the sorrows of life was *submission* — a good word, too, and one which played its heavy part in the old hymns, sermons and prayers. And yet, somehow I've never liked it. It has always to me had a weakly negative connotation. With it a picture forms in the mind of a human being, bowed down, crushed, impotent, like a slave beneath the master's lash. The other word of more recent use is *acceptance*. To me, at least, it suggests a different and more positive attitude, a sort of *taking into* our lives the disasters that befall us, the situations that distress us, even as we would take into our homes sometimes a necessary though most unwanted guest. And just as some have found that they have entertained angels unaware, so perhaps if we can only adjust adequately to our sorrows we may find some small grace, some little luster added to our characters.

A definition is likely to illuminate even the most familiar word so I checked with Webster on "acceptance." Here is what I found: *A receiving of what is offered with approbation, satisfaction OR acquiescence.* Of course no one but a completely other-world mystic could receive life's blows with satisfaction, but *acquiescence* is another matter. And here is the little gem, all unexpected, which I found almost hidden

among the other longer definitions. Mr. Webster had marked
it obsolete, though how any meaning of such shining and
eternal value could fall into disuse I cannot see. *Acquiesce: to
remain at rest in a place or mental state.* This seemed to me
to be the golden key to the whole matter, for if upon accepting life's troubles we can then remain *at rest* in our minds,
the battle has been fought and the victory won. But oh, it is
a hard battle and I, for one, have to wage it over and over.

So many people in great sorrow keep saying, "Why, *why*
did God send this upon *me?*" And because of the bitterness
underlying this question it is doubly hard for them to accept
what has befallen them. Would it not be better if they ceased
thinking that they were singled out by God for special pun-
ishment, and dwelt instead upon the fact that the universe
and our own small world are all subject to fixed and intricate
laws? The suffering that comes to us all usually happens because we or someone else, somewhere, sometime, interfered
with or broke one of these.

But while this latter attitude may remove from the heart
any hard or bitter feeling of injustice at God's hand, it need
never remove God from the situation itself. When the blow
falls, when the black grief strikes us, then it is that God enters
in. With that impelling racial intuition that seeks and finds a
Power greater than ourselves we reach up to Him and discover a strength upon which we can lean. David had plenty
of trouble in his life. As far as I can read, however, he accepted it, and he wrote for us his tender secret.

> Yea, though I walk through the Valley of the
>   Shadow of Death, I shall fear no evil;
> For thou art with me;
> Thy rod and thy staff, they comfort me.

And in *The Imitation of Christ* by Thomas à Kempis, there is this wonderful passage:

> My son, I am the Lord who giveth strength in the day of tribulation. This is what most of all hindereth heavenly consolation, that thou art too slow in turning thyself unto prayer. But do thou, having now recovered breath after the tempest, gather strength again in the light of my mercies; for I am at hand (saith the Lord) to repair all not only entirely but also abundantly and in most plentiful measure. Where is thy faith? Stand firmly and with perseverance; take courage and be patient; comfort will come to thee in due time. Wait, wait, I say, for Me. I will come and heal thee.

The line which I like best of all in this quotation is that which says: *But do thou, having now recovered breath after the tempest* . . . for in my own case, during the first utter desolation of sorrow, I couldn't even pray coherently.

There are so many emotional problems linked up with this matter of acceptance. There is, for instance, the whole wretched business of worry. This habit, which has seemed to become ingrained in the human race to its enormous detriment, is of course a result of man's material development. If we all lived a primitive outdoor life, basking in the sun by day, sleeping under the stars by night, with no concerns except food and physical love we would probably have never a worry, for that emotion is caused by unrest in one's present environment and unease about the future.

I will always remain convinced that much of the nervous tension (and certainly the digestive ills) of the human race comes from the fact that they got up on their hind legs too soon. If our Simian ancestors when their offspring first felt this urge had only said, "Easy now. Not too much of this all at once. You may take a little practice, walk on your hind legs a little each year but *no more* until at least eon after next!" Ah, if Mr. and Mrs. Simian had only enforced this plan with their ambitious young folks what perfect digestions we might have now! What unassailable nervous systems! And very likely how relatively little worry! For it may be that we have slipped up physically along the way and this has weakened our moral resistance. The eager, tumultuous spirit of man has galloped ahead of his weak flesh, has built him skyscrapers when he should have been digging caves, has fed him *pâté de foie gras* when he should have been gnawing bones.

But whether we should have arrived at the present stage of our development more slowly, the point is we are now here, in an age of the greatest complexity, of the atom bomb and the jet, of pressures, of artificiality, and above all of the most stupendous haste to get — where? Our bodies and minds are not properly geared to meet all this intensity, so we kick against the pricks.

It is sometimes almost as difficult to learn acceptance in connection with the constant, nagging little worries and the daily burdens of life as it is to do so after real tragedies. I speak here with the greatest feeling, for this is one of my besetting sins. I do worry. There are certain situations in my life which give me deep concern. How, I ask myself, can I *help* but worry? And yet I know, as we all do, that this eating, corrosive emotion saps the bodily strength and in a sense weakens the mind itself, for these disturbing thoughts crowd out more constructively happy ones. It is here that the picture of the ox helps me — the poor, troubled ox with his sore leg! If he could only have pulled his burden patiently, accepted it, as it were, told himself that after all things were not so bad; that he could still smell the rain and feel the sun and enjoy his dinner; that his kicking had only made himself more uncomfortable — this would have been the wise course.

In the case of the problems of life which give us worry I feel we should, of course, do all in our power to solve them; it is only with situations which cannot be altered that we should practice this grace of acquiescence which will help us remain "at rest" in our mental state.

One thing which all thoughtful people probably discover in connection with daily burdens and sharply pointed worries is that if they can just be patient, just hold on and wait for a time, the sharpness and the weight may disappear. All who know and love the sea will be familiar with a certain phenomenon which follows a "northeaster." For two or three days the wind has driven, the rain has poured and the ocean has risen and roared and lashed against the sands or the rocks. It would seem as though the dark fury of the elements would never pass. Then suddenly, as from one hour to the next, there comes a calm. The wind subsides, the rain stops, the ocean quiets. A faint manifestation of light is evident behind the leaden sky, while along the horizon there is an indescribably delicate diffusion of violet. It is not yet sunshine, but one knows the worst is over and before long the brightness of fair weather will return. So it is in life.

The reward for this calmness of mind, this patient waiting for the storm to pass was set forth long ago by Plotinus.

Let the soul banish all that disturbs; let the body that envelops it be still, and all the *frettings* of the body, and all that surrounds it; let earth and sea and air be still, and heaven itself. And then let man think of the Spirit as streaming, pouring, rushing and shining into him from all sides while he stands quiet.

And from Euripides these lines that are favorites of mine:

> What else is Wisdom? What of man's endeavor
> Or God's high grace so lovely and so great?
> To stand from fear set free, to breathe and wait.

Sometimes just "to breathe and wait" will turn a difficult situation into a bearable one.

One of the hardest burdens to accept, I think, is that of our own mistakes and their ensuing regrets or remorse. I am still startled by the contrast between life as actually lived and life as seen through the perspective of the later years. I, for example, see now with a crystal clarity the mistakes I've made, some small, some great, of which at the time I was quite unconscious. These haunt and distress me. Remorse is probably the inner soul's greatest sorrow. But this, too, must somehow be accepted and worked into the fabric of life. And for this I know no wiser words of balm than these of Brother Lawrence back in the seventeenth century which bear so beautifully, if obliquely, upon this particular anguish of the heart. They were written evidently to comfort those who were at times almost too ashamed of their own weaknesses and failures to pray.

> He lays no great burden upon us, a little remembrance of Him from time to time; a little adoration; sometimes to pray for His grace, sometimes to offer Him thanks for the benefits He has given you and still gives you in the midst of your troubles. He asks you to console yourself with Him as often as you can. Lift up your heart to Him even at your meals when you are in company; the least little remembrance will always be acceptable to Him. *You need not cry very loud; He is nearer than you think.*

And then there are — to name only two other areas of the heart's burdens — the great shattering disappointments to life's pattern, and the matter of physical disease and pain. These call for the greatest nobility of soul if they are to be accepted, if there is to be acquiescence. I often think with sheer wonder at the courage of the human heart! How can anyone possibly belittle mankind or feel that he is unworthy when his ability to rise above pain or sorrow is so phenomenal?

Years ago at a small luncheon I met a quiet woman who, without being gay or animated, yet took her pleasant part in the conversation. Afterwards I learned from my hostess that she was the mother of the young bride I had read of in the papers a year before, who had innocently opened her city apartment door to a window cleaner and been shockingly murdered. I, too, had a lovely young daughter. Could I, I asked myself then, could I have borne such a tragedy? And yet this woman was quietly going about her normal routine of living, intruding her grief upon no one.

I knew an editor once who went daily to his desk, doing his important work, laughing with his associates, advising and encouraging young writers, acting all the while as though he carried no inner secret, yet knowing that his days were numbered. I know now a distinguished writer who in the midst of great physical weakness and the loss of her eyesight works on steadily — if only an hour a day — at a new novel, and in between remembers to do kindnesses and dictate letters of lighthearted charm.

We all know countless examples of these courageous ones who have proved the truth of the words of Thomas à

Kempis: *If thou bear the Cross cheerfully, it will bear thee.*

I have thought so often, too, of the picture of the young men who, though full of the natural joy and hope of life, have gone uncomplainingly into battle. What moving, what magnificent acquiescence!

It seems to me that all these brave ones across the face of the earth have, by the triumph of their acceptance of disaster of every sort, cast a glory over the whole of mankind, a tender radiance, an illumination that throws its light upon us all in our time of need, and justifies men to God. "And remember," says the author of one of the Letters of the Scattered Brotherhood, "that the more tender, the more open, the gentler you can be in your quiet time of acceptance, of stillness, *the greater will be the power pressed through your silences.*"

Perhaps I should end with this sentence just written but I am impelled, in case it may be of help to someone, to add one little incident from my own experience even though it is in a sense anticlimactic, and even though it makes use of an entirely different metaphor from the one I used at the beginning of this chapter. My only excuse for this latter deviation is that in this most difficult and important problem of acceptance, I feel we need all the help (and all the metaphors!) we can get.

One evening a good while ago (when I had already planned this chapter) I happened to be greatly upset and distressed. I went out alone, my tears still wet upon my cheeks. I was walking beside the ocean, but suddenly I saw something very different from the sea. I had a startlingly clear picture of a quiet stream flowing gently between wooded banks. And from somewhere quite out of myself, it seemed, a sentence flashed into my mind: *Let the waters run softly!*

These words had immediate significance for me because I have been guilty at times of stirring up the stream of events with distress over the present, remorse for the past or anxiety for the future. In other words I suddenly saw how I had wrongly (even though with reason) muddied the stream and roiled it with these disturbing emotions. I wish this expression had come to me earlier but at least in practicing *acceptance* I am trying to use it now and I commend it to others.

Let the waters run softly, softly, without muddying them, softly under the bridge and on down the stream.

IV

The Two Approaches
to Life

"The people, therefore, that stood by, and heard it,
said that it thundered: others said, An angel spake to him."

THE GREAT LAW of diversity which enriches the physical world applies also to human personality. Just as no two grass blades are alike, according to the botanist, so, according to the psychologist, no two people react in the same way to given stimuli. Nature's infinite variety operates with such consummate skill that each unit of creation is distinctive and unique. A most exhilarating thought! But while this amazing fact is true of the human race there can still, of course, be divisions made and lines drawn, creating groups whose members in some general respect resemble each other while differing sharply from their opposites.

For example, on a long-ago day in the ancient capital of Judea, a city just then seething with political and religious dissension and crowded because of the great national feast, two kinds of people were gathered around a young prophet to hear what he had to say. He had already become famous

throughout the country because of the beauty and the fearlessness of his teaching — an idol of the crowds but a man
marked for death by the Temple party who did not like to
have their fundamental doctrines challenged. He had come
to the city for the feast, as did many of the devout, and as
was his own custom, even though it was an act of tremendous
courage to invade the stronghold of his enemies.

Now he stood in the street, speaking to the people before
him. He had barely uttered those remarkable words, "He
that loveth his life shall lose it; and he that hateth his life in
this world shall keep it unto life eternal," when a change apparently passed over his face. It was as though all at once he
ceased being objective; as though he no longer saw the crowd
about him, but felt only the weight of the danger threatening
himself. He was lost for a few brief moments in the tragedy
of his own fate, and his next words were wrung from his
inner self as though there were no listeners.

"Now is my soul troubled," he said, "and what shall I say?
Father, save me from this hour: but for this cause came I
unto this hour. Father, glorify thy name!"

And it was at this point that there was a sound in the
heavens above them. Most of the people present said it was
thunder; but there were a few who said it was an angel speaking to him.

Now I am not concerned with considering the validity of
either of these statements; I am interested only in the kind of
people who made them and in the quality of the personalities
they represented. For one of the great cleavages that divides
one element of mankind from another is that which separates
the sensitive, perceptive souls from the hardheaded, practical

ones. In the case of the crowd just referred to, I imagine that those who said that it thundered had been casting an eye now and then at the sky for some time. The weather was an important factor in connection with a feast then, as now. When they heard the thunder they would probably say in low tones to each other, "There it comes! I thought all day it looked like rain. Too bad! It will spoil things."

But the other group must have been looking only at Jesus' face as they listened to him, straining to catch every word. They had seen the sudden change come over him as he stopped preaching and wrestled with his own inner agony of fear; they had seen him overcome it, accepting his destiny. No wonder as they watched this drama in all its poignancy and power they thought the sound above them must be a celestial voice. I can picture them going back to their homes (or rooms if they were strangers in the city) changed in heart, never quite the same afterward because of what they had witnessed, stronger to overcome their own dark hours and commit all to God's keeping.

The other group of people, as they left the scene, were probably still discussing the weather.

So, there are these two different approaches to life: the one which takes note only of the fact itself; the other which sees behind the fact a significance, a beauty, a suggested meaning that transforms it, a wonder that infuses the common with the spiritual. The odd thing is that it is the latter group who usually come in for criticism, either sharp or good-natured. The completely practical people have always been likely to chide the dreamers as the striking example of Martha and Mary of Bethany bears witness. One can feel sympathy with Martha's annoyance that evening. She was "distracted," as the Revised Standard Version puts it, over getting the dinner and serving it when meanwhile her sister sat listening to Jesus, making no move toward the kitchen to help her. Martha complained rather bitterly to Jesus about this, but his answer was gentle, for he loved all that household.

"Martha, Martha," he said, "you are anxious and troubled about many things; one thing is needful. Mary has chosen the good portion, which shall not be taken away from her."

I imagine Martha was both hurt and annoyed at this; she probably banged the pots and pans a little then, and later had it all out with Mary after the guests had gone. But the major irritation that would remain in her mind was that Mary had something which could not be taken away from her. She had a hidden treasure, secret and safe, which Martha did not possess. Perhaps long afterward it would dawn upon her forthright soul that if she had not planned such an elaborate meal that evening she, too, might have had time to sit at the feet of their guest. The point to note is that she thought *only* of the dinner, while Mary thought only of Jesus' words.

There will probably always be mild conflict between these two groups: the one concerned with what they call *reality* and the other wandering at will in a world of bright and glowing intangibles. And because these latter people have a secret source of joy which the former cannot understand, the realists become a little critical, a little condescendingly arrogant, even a little sharp upon occasion, and all perhaps to cover up their sense of mystified alienation from a realm they do not know how to enter.

Now in this chapter I would like very humbly to speak first of the wonders of that world in which many people find deep pleasure, and second, to point out that while a sensitivity to beauty in all its manifestations is perhaps innate, yet it can be cultivated, and this conscious act of acquisition is one of the most important achievements in a life.

The ability to see beyond the fact is a queer thing. Now that I am set to speak of it, I hardly know how to begin. It arises, I think, from an inner joy, incommunicable but intense, which one experiences from the use of both the senses and the mind, in immediate perception or in the memory of it. Curiously enough, I had an example of the latter just after I had written the preceding paragraphs. I was tired and decided to drop my notebook and go into the garden. I pulled a few weeds and then stopped to examine some little lavender plants I had set out. They were still small, but tiny spikes of the authentic flower had appeared. I smelled them and then sitting down under a tree was completely transported.

Years ago my husband and I walked the pleasant distance from Stratford-on-Avon to Shottery, the home of Anne Hathaway. We went slowly through the house and then came out into the garden. There was a seat at the farther end and we went there, ignoring the busy "trippers," and sat down alone among the flowers. On long tables against the wall of the house great masses of lavender stalks lay drying in the sun. We sat on through a blissful hour, listening to the bees, smelling the rich fragrance, letting the magic circle of the years open wide to take us in.

We went to Evensong back in Stratford in the late afternoon, sitting in the choir stalls close to Shakespeare's grave in the chancel. The sunset light streamed through the high, richly colored window and fell across the altar and the stone slab. My heart was moved beyond expression to find myself kneeling in prayer, close, so close to the precious dust.

In the evening we rented a rowboat and drifted slowly in it down the river past the church, between the heavy green foliage on either side. There in the early dusk of the first stars I felt more than the mere beauty; more than the outward peace, lovely as that was. I felt Shakespeare's own thoughts moving . . . "I know a bank whereon the wild thyme blows," and ". . . Look how the floor of heaven / Is thick inlaid with patines of bright gold."

All this came back to me because of the scent of my little sprigs of lavender. The sense of smell has always been a great source of joy to me. The fragrance of apple blossoms in the spring, of lilacs after a rain, of honeysuckle on a warm June night, and the overpowering sweetness of locust bloom, which I particularly love — all of these move me indescribably. It is as though they were a concentration of life's most delicate happiness: first love, a springtime awakening of the soul, a draught of shyly dreamed-of, exotic delight, a union with beauty like the consummation of love itself. Once in my life, just once — and I remember the exact moment — I smelled the hot summer breeze blowing over a field of clover in bloom. I all but shuddered with the sweetness of it.

There are many sounds in nature, too, that stir me strangely. Of all bird notes, I would put first that of the thrush in the early evening, liquid, with longing and hope intermingled. The cicadas' strumming and chirring from the trees in the heat gives a very different effect certainly, but it brings me a sense of comfortable fulfillment. It comes in the summer's rich season, when gardens are ablaze, when harvests are being garnered, and when women in the country and small towns are setting their freshly made glasses of jelly to sun on window sills. I always feel a contentment, a repleteness, when I hear the cicadas, as I do also when I listen to the crickets' threnody in the fall. Their song means the end of summer, but it, too, has a comfortable, soothing iterance. If winter comes, there can still be a cricket on the hearth as the wood fire burns.

But of all nature's sounds I believe the most moving to me is that of the little frogs in the early spring. My husband and I used to drive out to the country each April just to hear them. From small streams and marshy meadows there arises this thin piping which seems to me to be the very quintessence of spring. "New *life!* New *life!* New *life!*" is the mysterious, sweet insistence of their song. It always gives me tremors in my soul. Happy ones.

These, of course, are only a very few of the sweet scents and sounds that happen to charm me. As to the pleasures of the eye, there is no limit! These are so constant to all who can see that there are few indeed who do not know a lift of the heart over some form of natural beauty. So, in the satisfactions of the sense of sight the two groups to which I have referred before come close to meeting. Even here, though, there is a difference in interpretation as Wordsworth stated with great clarity. He spoke once of a man to whom

> A primrose by a river's brim
> A yellow primrose was to him,
> And it was nothing more.

Then he said of himself in another poem:

> To me the meanest flower that blows can give
> Thoughts that do often lie too deep for tears.

The overpowering beauty of the world has always seemed to me to be one of the greatest proofs of the existence not only of a God, but of a personal one. The delicate, intricate, unendingly varied design in flowers and snowflakes, for example, seems to give the lie to a world of blind chance. The brilliantly lavish use of color alone does not seem compatible with mere pantheism. And I have always doubted whether the gorgeous protective stripes of the tiger and the zebra were arrived at without a *little* supervision! There is a sort of delicate humor, too, that pervades much of the loveliness of the earth: the pansy faces, the dandelion's frosty pate, the snapdragon's temper, the mayapple's umbrella. As Bryant puts it, there is a "smile" as well as eloquence of beauty, in Nature; and while she may seem at times to be "red in tooth and claw," there is surely plenty of evidence that another gentler and more personal force is at work.

One of my great delights has always been the moon, though I cannot tell why it affects me with such deep and extravagant pleasure. The first glimpse of it when it is a mere shaving of silver, a crescent whisper of light, stirs me with hope and happiness. Perhaps the ancients would have understood this feeling. They believed in the power of the moon over a human being. And, as a matter of fact, if the moon can affect the tide, drawing the mighty ocean to itself like a lover, why may it not in some way affect nature in general and even the hearts of men and women?

I had a dear old aunt who used to keep on the table beside

her chair a Bible, a prayer book, and the *Hagerstown Almanac*. She probably read them in that order during the winter, but I have an idea that in summer the almanac came out on top, for she was a great gardener and she planted everything according to the signs of the moon. My father was her despair, for he did his planting just when he felt like it. But Aunt Mary with the aid of the moon triumphed; her garden was always much better than ours. As she poured over the almanac's pages she could tell you just what phase of the moon was most propitious for weaning a baby, shingling a roof, or setting a hen. One thing even my father admitted: a field of wheat really *does* ripen in moonlight. This seems to me a lovely phenomenon.

My greatest lunar happiness has always come from the full moon, as is the case, I imagine, with all who love the moon at all. To see the rounded orb moving in majesty across the sky, showering pale radiance on all below, moves me to my very depths. The words of the poets always rise then to my mind:

> That orbèd maiden with white fire laden,
> Whom mortals call the moon . . .

> The moon, like a flower
> In heaven's high bower . . .

> Ah, moon of my delight
> That knows no wane!

And speaking of these quotations brings up the whole matter of poetry in general and the delicate art of the enjoyment of it. Coleridge wrote once that "poetry is the blossom and the fragrance of all human knowledge, human thoughts, human passions, emotions, language." And I would add to that definition the lovely lines of Keats: ". . . I will fly to thee, not charioted by Bacchus and his pards, / But on the viewless wings of poesy."

Poetry is truly the blossom and the fragrance *and the wings* of human thought. It is the poet who catches us up out of ourselves into a realm of new insight. It is he who gives us in distilled form the wisdom that underlies life and love and destiny. It is the poet who can not only feel our emotions but articulate them. "All the charm of all the Muses often flowering in a lonely word."

I have always loved poetry. As a child I was constantly making verses, and all through my teen years I continued, using the normal adolescent themes of sorrow, unrequited love and death. Why young people at this age should be absorbed creatively with these thoughts seems strange indeed, but any high school teacher of English will tell you this is so. I often recall now some verses I wrote when I was about sixteen. The first one ran:

> Be near me, Angel of Sleep!
> In the shadows before thee I lie,
> And beg but a glance from thy pitying eye,
> As the stars their watches keep.

Now, I ask myself, why did a completely happy young girl who slept every night like a top write this mournful appeal? The strange thing is that it has now, at my age, come quite sadly true. I frequently have need to cry for a blessing from the "Angel of Sleep," but how did the young girl of sixteen guess that feeling? Perhaps there is such a thing as age *pro*gression as well as age *re*gression. Do the young, especially those interested in some form of creative activity, catch a glimpse of experiences to come? I wonder.

However, not all my dirgelike ditties can be said to have been strictly prophetic of my later life. I remember the ending to one poem of which I was quite proud at the time. The lines were:

> Oh God, why should some have the bright summer day
> While I have the darkness of night!

As I recall, my mother was a little concerned over this effusion. During these years I copied in my best hand numbers of my "poems" and sent them off to magazines from the *Atlantic Monthly* down. The experience was good for me, for it inured me to rejections at a very tender age. But if my efforts did not find a place in the *Atlantic* they did occasionally find favor with the editor of the *Presbyterian Banner*, a religious weekly which came to our house. I don't think I have ever in many years of writing known such exquisite, intoxicating delight in publication as when the *Banner* printed a little poem, in lighter vein this time, when I was fifteen. To see it there in print over my initials (for some reason I had modestly withheld my name) was simply overwhelming. It was called "Black-eyed Susan" and I remember every word of it yet. It began:

> Roaming o'er the meadow grasses,
> Where the crimson clovers play,
> Lo, I come upon thee, Susan,
> Smiling there amongst the hay;
> Swaying, smiling,
> Me beguiling,
> Black-eyed Susan 'mongst the hay.

But while I was making verses in these formative years I

was also reading real poetry. Tennyson and Browning were my constant companions; and if I had now to choose the work of two poets for young people to feed upon I should choose these two, even though in this present year of grace the selection might be rated undistinguished by the moderns. The pure lyrical beauty and gentle mysticism of Tennyson, and the robust romanticism and inspired character delineation of Browning still seem matchless to me. So I read and dreamed over "The Princess" and "Love among the Ruins" and the rest, without realizing that I was entering a golden chamber in which ever after I was to "dwell, delighted."

For it is from the magic of poetry that a release of heart and mind may spring; the soul may feed upon a strange beauty, a shy beauty, that perhaps at first to the uninitiated only half reveals itself; but which gradually, if pursued, will open up a new world of wonder. There is the almost sensual pleasure in cadence and rhythm and the silver iterance of rhyme; but there is also the sudden revelation when we discover that we, too, can grasp the poet's insight which makes our own emotions and experiences universal instead of isolated.

Another familiar and yet celestial voice which breaks through the clouds of life is music. There are very few people who do not fall under the spell of some sort of music, from those who enjoy the tramping, tootling, country brass band to those who sit rapt at an opera or a symphony. The gift of music, too, is the most widely distributed of all the arts. To sing seems almost as natural for humans as for birds; and the ability to create music by mechanical means is tremendously widespread. So the enjoyment of it is almost uni-

versal, though here, also, as with the pleasures of the eye there
are wide differences in degree and quality. For those who can
appreciate the finest forms of music where theme and tone
become rarefied there is surely to be found a peculiar rapture.

In my native village, music played an important part in our
lives. Our own home was always full of it, for my mother
and father both possessed good natural voices and loved to
sing. My mother sang at her work; my father sang songs of
his native Scotland around the winter fire. At our young
parties, too, the boys and girls crowded around the piano and
sang for their own entertainment. On great occasions such as
Decoration Day and the Fourth of July, the town band performed. I can still see its members marching stoutly up Main
Street with a Civil War veteran leading with his fife. He was
a tall man, heavily built, and he swayed impressively from
side to side as he played expertly his notes of shrill and pierc-
ing beauty.

Another type of music which still returns to me often in
memory was the singing of the Twenty-third Psalm at
funeral services which were then always held at the home.
To hear the slow blending of voices, especially on the summer air, as they rose unaccompanied, the women's from inside
the house, the men's from the yard without, in a simple
diapason of faith, was moving indeed.

While music of some sort was interwoven closely with all
the events of life, both of joy and sorrow, and while many
people in the town had a natural gift for it, we had one real
musician in our midst. This was Miss Bessie. She had "gone
away to school" in her youth, studied music, taught it for
some years in a girls' seminary, and then come home to keep

house for her bachelor brother who was a farmer. He was
not what we call a "gentleman farmer," but he lived like a
gentleman; and certainly Miss Bessie, whose expressive hands
had worked upon many a print of butter as well as upon the
keyboard, would have been at home in any drawing room
anywhere, for she had both dignity and charm. When she
sat at the great old-fashioned piano in her parlor, her talent
became manifest.

At all large parties the high moment came when Miss Bessie
was led forward to render "The Brook." This selection was
not a classical one, certainly, but it was a charming (and difficult) accompaniment for Tennyson's poem of that name.
As she played and sang, Miss Bessie's hands moved over the
keyboard with incredible dexterity. But this was not all. She
made us *hear* the brook: the soft plash and gentle ripple; the
"fretting" over stones, and chatter of its many "sharps and
trebles"; then the surge and flow as it joined the brimming
river. I have heard a number of great pianists since, but for
sheer interpretative imagery, I have never heard anyone who
surpassed Miss Bessie with "The Brook."

After my marriage, music became even more important to
me because of my husband's taste and love for it. We had
many great moments at the opera or at concerts; we had many
more happy everyday ones when we listened to records or
tried in our extremely limited fashion to create music with
flute and piano. Not even our blundering could wholly
destroy the beauty of Gluck's *Orpheus*, for example, and
sometimes we were conscious of a real exaltation when we
had done passably well.

I have always been amazed at the great diversity of musical

compositions in respect to their power to affect the listener. For instance, of all the music I have ever heard I believe I have been most profoundly moved, most "caught up in a vision" by Verdi's *Requiem*. And yet at the other end of the scale I have felt stirred almost to tears when I have heard young men singing (especially in wartime) the popular "Whiffenpoof Song":

> Gentlemen songsters off on a spree
> Bound from here to eternity . . .

The plaintiveness of the tune which matches the tragic and youthful significance of the words.

So my taste is certainly catholic. Yet here, indeed, may lie music's greatest charm: its almost universal appeal, its unbelievably wide range. It rises to heaven; it broods beside the cottage door; it gives a voice to joy or sorrow; it releases tightly bound emotions and lets us laugh and weep and hope again; in short, it brings the indescribable beauty of melody into our lives.

But now, having mentioned rather discursively, I fear, a few of the pleasures that lie in that world behind the hard material fact, I would like to consider for a moment how one may enter it. To some the way is natural and instinctive; to others it seems an impossible passage into an alien land. The most important thing to remember is that while the most sensitive and perceptive souls make the approach fairly easily, even they do not go far without some conscious effort. In other words, the art of *appreciation* is one that must be constantly developed, constantly cultivated. The wise old saying that "the appetite grows by what it feeds upon" is never more true than when applied to the enjoyment of literature, music and art. When a man finds no pleasure in books, either poetry or prose, this situation can definitely be cured by his *making* himself read something from the world's best authors. If he persists, the "appetite" for reading will come and grow and he will soon be lost in a wider and more fascinating world. If a woman has no taste whatever for good music and no interest in art in any form, she can still enter these magic regions if she will deliberately set herself, for example, to listen to fine records, which are easily available, and also *take* herself, *make* herself go to the nearest art gallery. Here, if she saunters slowly through, feasting her eyes upon the masters, a new delight will be born in her. A new door will open, and she will even view herself with fresh respect.

We are not likely to care for or be interested in that about which we know nothing, but any knowledge gained is always a pleasurable acquisition. Our stature increases; we have a warm feeling of kinship with many new things and new people — a result which brings deep satisfaction.

I am most concerned in all this matter with the lives of young people who are establishing their first homes. Most boys and girls in their college years experience a stimulation of mind and usually an active interest in some form of the creative arts. But when they marry and the responsibilities of a home and a family settle upon them this mental eagerness sometimes becomes dulled. Besides this, the young people of this generation have a fascinating Enemy which can in certain respects ruin their capacity for appreciation. This is television.

Now, I frankly admit at once that I have a T.V. set myself and greatly enjoy many of its programs, but it does present a problem in self-discipline even to me at my age in that its danger is insidious. Television is hypnotic; it is soporific. It demands nothing of us. As a rule the mind's defense rests as we watch it. Sometimes this can be a therapeutic boon, but not too often. The danger is that we sit glued to it without exercising any selective faculty whatever. And *this* is what I fear in the case of young people. When the youthful father cames home tired from the day's work, when the young mother sits down at last to relax after dinner, dishes, and getting the babies to bed, it is so terribly easy to turn the dial and slump down to watch whatever happens to be on the screen, whether interesting or drab, and to continue doing this until it becomes the regular indiscriminate pattern of their evenings.

Then there are the children who are growing up with this new and to them delightful Monster. When my daughter was a young thing we as parents were all greatly concerned about the effect of the movies upon children. As I look back upon it now, how relatively simple that problem was. At least it was controllable. It was on the outside. But television is enshrined in the heart and center of the average home. While the mother is busy in another room, a young child may flip the dial and witness scenes of noisy violence and criminal bloodshed before anyone else is aware. This seems to me a most serious situation with possibly far-reaching and pernicious results.

There are many delightful programs for children, those coming in the late afternoon being a heaven-sent gift to the busy mother; but it requires great determination and vigilant supervision on the part of the parents to hold the children to the entertainment suited for their years. One couple I know have solved the problem by refusing to have television in their house. "If we do," the father said, "I'm afraid our girls will not *read*."

So, if I could speak to all the young people whom I know, and those whom I do not, I would give this most urgent advice: don't allow the thunder of mediocrity to drown out the celestial voices in your homes. Don't let yourselves sink into a welter of the commonplace. Turn off television for one or two evenings a week and read a good book; listen to beautiful music; gather about you a few friends whom you have deliberately chosen because they enjoy fine things too. Make an effort to cultivate your taste along the line of all the creative arts so that your children will enjoy the rich heritage of a cultural background.

But now there remains one other consideration, the greatest of all. I have spoken of a certain approach to life by which we may enjoy beauty in its varied forms. For myself, I know that I love, almost with passion, the physical beauties of the universe; I crave constantly the nourishment I find in poetry, the solace of music, and the inspiration of art, especially sculpture, which Mme. de Staël called "stationary music." I have for all these a certain degree, at least, of mature appreciation. But in the realm of spiritual perception I am still a stumbling child. So much of the time I hear the thunder instead of the angel's voice. I am Mary today, and Martha tomorrow.

One great problem for most of us, I believe, is how to achieve that spiritual versatility which will color all we do with golden light. Angela Morgan sang of this quality when she wrote her beautiful poem, "Kinship."

I am aware,
As I go commonly sweeping the stair,
Doing my part of the everyday care —
Human and simple my lot and my share —
I am aware of a marvelous thing:
Voices that murmur and ethers that sing
In the far stellar space where cherubim sing . . .
I am aware,
As I sit quietly here in my chair
Sewing or reading or braiding my hair
Human and simple my lot and my share . . .
I am aware of the splendor that ties
All the things of the earth with the things
    of the skies,
Here in my body the heavenly heat,
Here in my flesh the melodious beat
Of the planets that circle Divinity's feet
As I sit silently here in my chair,
I am aware.

This feeling of kinship with the universe, this feeling of *awareness* of the close tie existing between "the things of the earth" and "the things of the skies," comes only, I believe, with practice.

In the olden days a very definite rule for achieving this illumination of the spirit was repeated frequently. It was this: "Make diligent use of the means of grace." These last words always impressed me for surely *grace* is the most beautiful benediction that can fall upon a human soul.

The *means* were three: the church, the Bible, and prayer. One interesting thing to note about them is that they are usable by people of every faith; and although their practice is very old it has never, I believe, been supplanted by anything better. In our present troubled age the "diligent" use of these

means might make all the difference in a life between confusion and order, between despair and peace.

The church, any church, has two great gifts to offer: first,
the stimulus and spiritual support of common worship; and
second, the intangible quality of holy restfulness. Pascal
said that most of the evils of life arose from "man's being
unable to sit still in a room." In church we sit still. We relax
in the quiet of a sacred place. This is good for us.

Then there is the Bible, described by scholars as our greatest piece of literature. It is that, of course, but it is much
more. It is a dramatic record of man's search for God. To
those who are unfamiliar with it, the fiercely exciting records
of the Old Testament with their lusty language may come as
an interesting surprise. Certainly every child has a right to
know the story of the little Moses in the bulrushes, of
Joseph's coat of many colors, of Daniel in the lion's den, and
of David and Goliath. These and many others are more
thrilling than anything he will find on T.V. They are also
part of a great religious heritage which no child should be
allowed to miss, just as no ardent young man or woman
should miss the exotic beauty of the Song of Solomon.

> Whither is thy beloved gone, O thou fairest
>   among women?
> Whither is thy beloved turned aside? that
>   we may seek him with thee.
> My beloved is gone down into his garden,
>   to the beds of spices,
> To feed in the gardens and to gather lilies. . . .
>
> Many waters cannot quench love,
> Neither can the floods drown it."

And for us all there is comfort and guidance in the Psalms, the Sermon on the Mount and St. Paul's magnificent thirteenth chapter of First Corinthians ("Though I speak with the tongues of men and of angels . . .") to mention only these few selections.

Whether in the Old Testament or in the New there is food for the spirit and the mind also. Anyone who in his reading has missed (or is missing) the Bible, has an impoverished life. To put it affirmatively, all who make themselves familiar with the Bible will find their lives enriched and strengthened.

There are of course other lesser books of devotion which are helpful to one striving for this spiritual illumination. For myself I would put first in this group *The Imitation of Christ* by Thomas à Kempis. Many times over the years when I have felt discouraged by my own failings I have read his words and been comforted. "Remember," he says, "thou art man, not God; thou art flesh, not an angel." There is scarcely an experience of the soul that he does not know and describe with tenderness, adding his good counsel. His chapter on love I have always felt could worthily stand beside that of St. Paul himself.

> Love watcheth, and sleeping, slumbereth not. Though weary, love is not tired; though pressed, it is not straightened; though alarmed, it is not confounded; but as a lively flame and burning torch, it forces its way upwards, and securely passeth through all. If any man love, he knoweth what is the cry of this voice.

Another book of devotion which I have found helpful in recent years is *Letters of the Scattered Brotherhood*. These letters, edited by Mary Strong, are, we are told, records of the genuine spiritual experience of various people and are not contributions written originally for a journal or book. They have the unusual combination of mysticism and practical advice and give one a constant feeling of uplift.

The third "means of grace" is prayer, that most mysterious link between man and God. This cry of the human soul to its Creator is universal and instinctive. Everybody prays, consciously or unconsciously, in times of emergency; but as a means to spiritual growth I believe habitual prayer is necessary. Here again there is demanded of us some effort — not in the act of praying itself, for as Brother Lawrence says, "You need not cry very loud; He is nearer than you think" — but in making the time for regular prayer. It is true that communion with God can take place anywhere at any hour; but my own experience has been that if the practice of prayer is left to vague and uncertain times it is likely to be omitted altogether. On the other hand, if even a few minutes each day are regularly devoted to prayer — when we first wake in the morning or before we fall asleep at night, for instance — we are sure to find strength, guidance and consolation, and the realization that this faithful habit is indeed binding us "with gold chains about the feet of God."

And so there are the two approaches to life: one in which the mind and spirit see nothing beyond the fact, the tangible, the commonplace, if you will; the other in which there is perceived all those forms of beauty which lie beyond the easily discernible and which bring exultation both to the senses and to the soul. If we crave this exultation, if we try earnestly to cultivate it, then the celestial voices will come to us instead of the thunder, with grace and with an indwelling reality.

V

The Obligation of
the Impossible

"Be ye therefore perfect."

IT IS A LONG TIME since I first thought about this command to perfection, and even then, young as I was, I had a faint feeling of superior wisdom as I considered it. I knew better than to take this seriously; I knew that perfection in any line was the one great impossibility in this world; so the thing to do was to set the words down as suggestive hyperbole and let them go at that. And through all the years until quite recently this has been my attitude. Then one day I made a discovery. Something lies plainly in the context of this line for all to read, and yet I had never noticed it before. The revelation which came so startlingly to me was that this strange command deals with *love*. It is as though the Great Teacher had said, "Be ye therefore perfect *in love*." This set me upon a new and, to me, most interesting line of thought.

One of the first lessons a child has to learn is that he is hedged about with limitations, that the impossible confronts

him at every turn and, though he does not yet realize it, that
his safety and his very survival depend upon his conforming
to the limital bounds. As he grows older the boundaries re-
cede, but they are still there. He constantly meets conditions
which to him are contrary to the nature of reality, or, as we
say, impossible. In relation to his physical entity, therefore,
perfection of correspondence with his surroundings is unat-
tainable. It is sad that this should be so, for the human body,
developed during eons of evolutionary processes, is surely the
greatest of earth's wonders.

But though this is true, and in spite of the fact that medical
research has so greatly reduced disease and lengthened the
span of living, the body never reaches *perfection* of function
and so cannot survive the eventual deterioration of the years
and the final catastrophe.

When we turn from thinking of man's body to considering
his *unconquerable mind*, it would seem we were more nearly
approaching the possibility of perfection, for here we enter
what Goethe calls "the inner universe" where physical limits
disappear and the intellectual horizon is endless. But the point
is that even here there *is* a horizon beyond which stretches
the infinite and unencompassable sea of ideas, of pure ration-
ality, science and imagination. This age in which we live is a
dangerous one in which to employ negation. The apparently
impossible happens every day, yet something beyond always
beckons, always eludes. It might perhaps be true to say that
the mass mind of men will at some far future time reach a
perfection of knowledge. Even this I doubt. Certainly it is
true that no individual, however massive his intellect, has yet
reached either rational or artistic perfection. The stress of

the reach, the craving grasp, which are in themselves the very essence of development, still fail of complete attainment, of the consummation hoped for. No one reaches the ultimate height; each drops below the peak toward which his mind has striven.

This is true, of course, of every creative artist; but it is the valid experience of every mental worker, of every scientist and scholar, great or small, and also of every average man who feels his mind beating against the bars of the unknown.

There is left, then, only one area of life's experience in which to seek for the ideal of perfection; this is in the realm of emotion. Now, at first thought this may seem not only strange, but foolish, for this of all man's faculties is usually regarded as the most volatile, the most unstable. Yet when we consider more carefully we find this judgment is incorrect.

The truth is that the essential emotions of joy, grief, hate and love have changed little through all man's slow and devious progress. Emotions become rarefied as we ascend the scale of development but basically they have remained the same during every human age and condition. Indeed we may say they represent the one constant in the flux of the years. And of all the emotions the deepest, the greatest of these is — love.

There remains then to consider whether there can be such a thing as perfection in love. The more I have thought of this the more convinced I am that it is not only possible, but practicable; and that the basis for this perfection is unselfishness. These key words are in such ordinary use that their strength and full import are likely to be weakened. Love is, as the popular song says, "a many-splendored thing," but it is also a very complex thing in that its types vary so widely that the word itself seems to grow a bit commonplace. Unselfishness is known, of course, as a virtue, but here, too, the bright patina of its significance becomes dulled by casual use of the term. It is only when we allow an intense light to play upon the relation between *love* and *unselfishness* that the ideal of perfection emerges.

In all the ages the purest love known has been that of a mother for her child. Here is an example of absolute selflessness. The child and its welfare are the mother's supreme interest, no matter what the cost to herself. To paraphrase the wonderful passage on love from *The Imitation* to which I have referred before, she feels no burden, thinks nothing of trouble, attempts what is above her strength, she watcheth, and sleeping, slumbereth not. Her fierce protectiveness, her utter devotion to the object of her affection have made mother love a symbol, whether we have thought of it so or not, of *perfection*.

Parental love, then (for I would put the father's emotion very close to that of the mother) has perhaps already proven the point in question. Of course there are some selfish parents in the world; there are those who want the pleasure and pride of parenthood without the steady sacrifice and care which is essential; there are those who hold their children too tightly, for their own pleasure alone; there are those strange hearts which are callous because of inner distortion or outer hardships; but certainly the great rule runs true in spite of the exceptions. The primitive, instinctive mother love through all the ages has been rooted, apparently, in the biological processes of a woman's very being and Nature helps her to achieve this perfection almost without effort.

But to rise to perfection in love in all the other areas of life is not so instinctive and therefore not so easy. For example, the opposite of the parents' love for their children is that of children for their parents. Here, it seems to me, we run into a serious problem. Just as it is natural for a father and mother to give and give, so it is at first essential and later habitual for the children to take and take. And this is right, except when the giving is too great and the taking too casual.

I once, years ago, knew a fine man and woman with one gifted young son. The husband's salary was small; their home was modest but charming and they dearly loved it. They sold the house to send the son to college. They did it with the high-minded generosity of the true lady and gentleman, and the son accepted it rather easily. I have often thought of this since. I believe the sacrifice was too great. The son should have said, "Never! You mustn't give up our home. I'll try for a scholarship. I'll work my way through somehow. Plenty of boys do. We'll find a solution."

But how can young people be taught unselfishness? This boy was not unusual. Almost any youth will accept a sacrifice for a desired boon, if it is pressed upon him. Out of the fullness of their love parents are likely to increase the normal selfishness of their children. I adored my own mother and father. Anything that is good in me I owe to them. Although they have now been gone long years there is hardly a passing day when I do not think of them, seeing them vividly as they were, remembering the happiness we knew together, hearing their laughter, feeling their love still upon me. To me they were perfect; yet this strange thing is true. I believe I would all my life have been a better woman if they had *taught* me to be unselfish. I had their own example constantly before me, but one's eyes are likely to be dulled a little to that which one sees daily. I needed actual precept too. And this is where most parents feel a hesitancy. It is very difficult to say, "You, my precious child, should do thus and thus *for us*." And yet in default of such training many young people are missing a perfection of love which would develop their characters and give them deep satisfaction as their lives progress.

It is a delicate tightrope here that parents have to walk. To them the greatest joy is to give without thought of themselves; but at a point they should, I think, make sure that their children have a chance to exercise their own unselfish thoughtfulness, even to the point of small sacrifices.

It is easy to think of simple examples to illustrate this. In the average home where the requirements of a growing family constantly strain the budget, it is almost certain that the mother will do without new clothes in order that her daughter may be prettily dressed, and the father may decide his old tweed suit will see him through another winter in order that Bud in college may have a new tux for the prom. This is natural as breathing for the parents, and right also. Certainly any normal mother will get more genuine pleasure in buying an evening gown for her daughter than in adding to her own wardrobe. But there should be a point at which the tables are turned. Suppose there comes a time when the mother really *needs* a new winter coat and the daughter greatly wants one whether she needs it or not. Perhaps then they could talk the matter over. The mother could say, "I'm terribly sorry, Mary, but I'm afraid I'll have to be the one to get a coat this year. Won't you come with me soon and help me select it?"

By the time Mary has gone shopping with her mother, watched her pleasure in the purchase, seen how elegant she looked in it, listened later as she tells her friends how much she depends upon Mary's taste, the girl will have a new glow in her heart, a new respect for herself and a new experience in unselfishness. She will be a jot nearer perfection in her love for her mother.

I remember distinctly a morning some years ago when I had had a delightful mail I met a woman whose daughter, like mine, was in college. "Oh, how is ———," I asked eagerly. The mother's face clouded. "I really don't know too much about her," she said. "She hardly ever writes."

The unfortunate thing about this girl's selfishness was that both she and her parents suffered from it. Their hearts were hurt of course by her lack of thought for them. They missed her presence enough in all conscience without losing also the link that would have brought her near even in their separation. But the girl, too, was losing something: the peculiar joy of *giving* to her parents the one important gift in her power, and, through the lack of that, missing a certain stability of character which would have come to her from clearly recognizing a duty and converting it into a pleasure.

It is normal for young people in every generation to have an intense preoccupation with themselves, their own interests, their own pleasures, the carrying out of their own desires. In other words it is natural for us all when we are young to be unconsciously selfish; and sometimes that tendency becomes rooted.

I have wondered if it might not be possible for young

fathers and mothers to combat this danger by starting to teach unselfishness to their children when they are very young. All well-bred parents begin to teach good manners to their off-spring from the cradle (since these are necessary to pleasant living and an outward sign of inward grace); obedience and truthfulness and honesty, the cardinal virtues of childhood, are also instilled early and persistently. If unselfish thought-fulness for others were deliberately taught day by day, not just casually suggested, this ideal of perfection might be more easily attained in maturity.

I have the greatest sympathy with young people, remem-bering myself at their age. Youth is a time of such utter optimism, such confidence in the future, such happy igno-rance of the coming vicissitudes of life! No wonder the eyes of youth are filled with the joy of their own pursuits, and that it is difficult for them to see what goes on in the lives of their parents and even of their brothers and sisters. Their apper-ception is marginal, not inclusive.

When young people marry, the love between parents and children may suffer certain strains. Probably no happy young bride on her wedding day realizes what brightness she is removing from her parental home. This is the way of the world; this is the way it must be from grandmother to mother to daughter and to that daughter's daughter. The radiant young thing must go off on the arm of her husband and her parents must laugh and be gay and wave her goodbye with their blessing — and then come back to the home that has lost its chief reason for being. From then on the girl's first al-legiance must be to this young stranger; the father and mother who have been up till then the center of her life must take second place. This is right, this is inevitable, and — this is painful for the parents. For those of the young man also, of course, there is this sense of loss. No more will they hear the boy tearing up the stairs, singing loud hit tunes in the shower, bringing in other young males to pound the piano, or have sessions by the fire, or raid the icebox. All the hilarious jokes of the growing-up years will be remembered with a pang. "Hi, Beautiful!" to his mother. "Go out with me sometime?" Or to his father, "Sorry, sir, but there's a slight economic depression in the region of my pants pocket!"

There is a difference now. The carefree boy is married, the head of a new home, a husband, perhaps, in a year or two, a father.

Now, because of these natural changes which are a necessary part of life, there are adjustments to be made on both sides. The parents of both girl and boy must learn to relinquish gracefully. There will be mistakes, the number varying in direct proportion to the closeness of the tie before; but they must patiently practice unselfishness; they must not be possessive; they must still cover their own child, and their new child, with the mantle of their love, but without smothering them in their new freedom. Last Sunday I heard a sermon that touched my heart. At the end of it the minister leaned upon the pulpit and said simply, "To sum it up, *be kind, be tender!*" This seems to me the perfect admonition for parents at all times but certainly in this their new role.

A short time ago I attended a dinner party at which all the men and women at table were parents of grown children. The talk suddenly turned upon the subject of giving advice to married sons and daughters. The conversation was at once animated in the extreme. One woman said advice should *never* be given unless it was asked for. (I have known many other parents who made this their inflexible rule.) But the majority of those at that table, of whom I made one, disagreed almost violently with this attitude. One man cited an instance in which he had most urgently advised his son-in-law to hold on to his government life insurance. The father said his advice had not been asked for and probably never would have been, but he *knew* the course of action he suggested was for the young man's best good, and that of his daughter too, and he could not have rested if he had not given his judgment.

The conversation ended with this majority opinion: Since parents of older children have already lived most of their lives, it is natural to assume that they have learned some valuable lessons, something in the way of wisdom. If they deliberately refrain from passing this maturer outlook on to their young people just because the latter are married, then they are denying their children a certain help which may indeed be more important to them than financial aid. The element of unselfishness, strangely enough, enters in here also. Young people, when grown, do not always relish advice. They may indeed be a trifle annoyed by it even when it is given as it always should be, gently and kindly and only occasionally. So, in a sense, it would be much easier for parents to do nothing in this matter. But that attitude, to me, is just a little like that of a mother who lets her child handle a dangerous object because she knows he will be irritated at her if she takes it away from him.

One voice was raised at that dinner party which drew laughter from the entire table.

"But do they ever thank you for your advice? Do they ever tell you afterwards that you were right?" one of the men asked.

As I say, everyone laughed. And yet there was a hint of wistfulness in the laughter; which brings us to consider the young peoples' opportunity for perfection in their role of married children. To most young men and young women, brought up in a happy home, articulate with love, the carrying over into their married lives of their constant devotion to their parents is a natural and inevitable thing. The early years of marriage, however, do bring certain peculiar problems to the bride and groom. There is now a double set of parents to be considered. Happy the young couples who have *two* friendly and loving families to be interested in all their welfare! But, unfortunately this ideal situation does not always occur. The girl may not "take to" her mother-in-law; the young man may conceive a dislike of his new father. Since there is youth on the one side there is likely also to be a certain independence, a tendency to carry a proud chip on the shoulder. But because they *are* young the bride and groom can afford to be generous. The riches of long coming years are theirs. The parents' time, alas, may not be too long. The beauty and hope of youth are strong possessions. Wrapped in their own secure joy in each other it would be relatively easy to practice upon the in-law who is giving trouble an unselfish thoughtfulness. Love is the most disarming thing in the world. It can break down stouter barriers than the friction in families. Nothing costs less or gives greater rewards.

I have known cases where there has been complete estrangement between married children and their parents. This seems to me sheer tragedy. The blame sometimes can be evenly divided; but wherever it lies there should be the utmost effort on both sides to bring about reconciliation. There is no room here for pride, so if this effort must all be on *one* side, then so it must be.

While there may be no open breach, there is often hidden pain. Take for example the case of the young man who is an only child and naturally the life and center of his home. He marries into a large family who accept him with warmth. The girl, devoted to her people, perhaps unconsciously draws her husband almost completely into her own wide circle, leaving his father and mother lonely and saddened in many ways. The same, of course, may happen if it is the girl who is the only child, and the young man one of a large and lively family.

Certain other situations which happen constantly are those in which a girl, born with the silver spoon, reared in wealth, marries a youth who has nothing to offer but his own worth and ambition; or in which a young man from a socially elect home marries a girl from a simple background; or in which two young people of different religious faiths fall in love and marry. In a society such as ours these relationships are bound to occur continually, but even though they impose additional difficulties, love can conquer, for it recognizes no social, economic or religious barriers. One of my closest friends came from a very wealthy family; when quite young she married the then impecunious young man of her choice. She tells an amusing story of her early married days. Her mother called to see her one morning and found her on her knees in the kitchen.

"Mother!" the new bride exclaimed with a tragic gesture, "*I'm scrubbing the floor!*"

"Yes," her mother answered calmly, "and I've never seen you look better in your life!"

What a wise mother! How easily she could have cast a cloud over her daughter's marriage if she had cried out instead, "Oh, my *poor child!*"

In the case of so-called mixed marriages, I can cite several concrete happy examples. In each case the young man is a Roman Catholic and the girl a Protestant. Due to an arbitrary rule of the Roman church, the children of these unions must be brought up in their father's faith. Now, if he made this faith dominant in the home, to the extent of completely ignoring that of his wife who gave their children birth and whose blood flows equally with his in their veins, this would be an attitude not only of extreme selfishness on his part but of grave danger. Sometime, perhaps when least expected, this behavior would be sure to cause resentment and perhaps serious unhappiness. In the cases of which I am thinking, however, the condition is different. The young man in each *respects* his wife's faith; there is no constraint on this subject; she speaks as freely in the home of her religious affiliation as he does of his. In fact one young husband I know takes his wife to her own place of worship on Sunday and calls for her there although he goes with the children to his church at another hour. This mutual tolerance and open respect for each other's religious allegiance, which is based upon unselfishness, will insure the perfection of their love in this more or less difficult situation.

So in all cases where the backgrounds of young people are

different, a constant thoughtfulness on the part of all concerned is the only sure means of alleviating the additional
strains which such circumstances impose upon both the married children and their fathers and mothers.

But while this striving for perfection in love should take
place on the part of parents and children, brothers and sisters,
relatives and friends, it is essential that it operate in the closest
and most intimate of all human relationships — that of husband and wife. For in this love there enters something god-
like and creative; in this union there lies something of profound urgency; it is through the strange and rapturous act of
sex that new life is born.

The marvel of this should stop us dead in our tracks!
Emerson says that if the stars shone only one night in a year,
men would look and marvel. So should we look upon this
process of creation with reverence and wonder, for the love
which causes it is made up of mysterious elements: enchant-
ment, passion, devotion, transport, the very flame of life itself. Is it not necessary then that there should be *perfection*
in its fulfillment? And is it not unspeakably sad that so often
it falls short of this ideal?

The normal prelude to the married estate is one of the most
admired phenomena in the world: young love. The strong,
eager virility of the boy, the tender, budding beauty of the
girl, represent Nature's undeviating design for the continuance of the race. The young lovers do not know it but
they are propelled to each other's arms by laws as strong as
those that hold the stars in their courses. And because they in
themselves represent this most delicate and springlike phase of
happiness, they are the center of tender regard by high and

low. "All the world loves a lover." Disillusioned old men look upon them with a mist in the eye; the worn faces of older women soften with a fleeting look of youth; the middle-aged smile wistfully, remembering. For at this stage in the minds of the young lovers there is but one thought: "For ever wilt thou love, and she be fair!"

Now while it is inevitable that life must work its will upon all of us, gradually changing the physiognomy and teaching the heart to bear sorrow, pain and care, I am convinced in spite of all statistics that in the vast majority of cases the love that begins in this way between husband and wife does continue; it abides; it even grows stronger through the years. This does not mean, however, that the guardians of love do not both need to exert the most careful and constant effort to preserve the beauty of it and to bring it to perfection.

The curious thing is that while there are always large moments of failure in this regard, perhaps the greatest threats are "the little foxes," the little hurts and disappointments that cause married happiness to be impaired. Sex, that most mysteriously beautiful fact which draws husband and wife together and of them makes one flesh, also presents a subtle barrier between them. He will always be essentially man; she, essentially woman. Their reactions to all life's experiences, small as well as large, will be colored and controlled by this difference.

Women are more easily hurt than men. So many little things can stab them: a hasty word, a straying glance, a breach of remembrance, an unexpected criticism. Of course to counterbalance this, most wives are also made happy by little things: a touch, a kiss, an unusual endearment or word of praise, a flower, an unexpected gift. But there is this fundamental difference between the hurts of a wife and those of her husband. As I have said, the woman is wounded more easily, but when she is unhappy she can weep. She can be articulate. She can say to the man (in Browning's words), "Just this or that in you offends me." Even though at times half mystified, he will in all probability soothe her; her tears will be dried and she will fall asleep that night in his arms, comforted.

But when a man is hurt he cannot cry. Those particular tears which afford a woman release would be blood-drops from his heart. They would destroy his manhood. He dare not weep. And it is likely that he will not even mention the thing that has hurt him. This too, to a man, would seem beneath his dignity. Instead, he will show his feelings obliquely which may completely confuse his wife. He will lose his temper over an inanimate object; he will grow irritable or he will become silent. In any case the thorn in his breast will not have been removed. It will be pressed down within him. Which means, I think, that while women are more easily hurt, men are more deeply vulnerable.

I have often wondered if the enormous number of heart ailments among men might be partly due to the inhibited emotion which our society requires of its male members. I believe if men dared cry as women do, without loss of respect, they would live longer. Maybe it is the many little repressed pains in their hearts that cause the last incurable one. And yet — this thought has just come to me — if they wept easily and often, their tears, now rare, would then mean no more than those of a woman. Some years ago I was given an honorary degree by a certain college. As I stood up to receive it and be invested with the hood, my husband in the audience had tears running down his cheeks. Oh, to think that my little moment of honor meant so much to him that he would *weep* for me! That is one of my most precious memories which I shall carry in my heart until I die.

The physiological difference between a man and a woman accounts for some of the hurts that wives sustain. A normal woman is by nature monogamous. It is easy for her to be faithful to one man. Although I believe sincerely that the great majority of husbands are as faithful as their wives, one must admit the fact that a male is also acutely conscious of feminity in general. He notices a woman's pretty face much more often than his wife turns to look at a handsome man. In her vast amoral wisdom, Nature has seen to it that most women, especially in youth, are attractive and desirable. Now a man may notice these qualities with pleasure, a purely superficial and quickly forgotten delight, and still be an utterly loyal and devoted spouse, but if I could, I would give all husbands this advice: look at every pretty face if you will; admire every shapely leg if you must, only *keep quiet about it* in your wife's presence. For no woman, no matter how calm and wise she may seem to be on the surface about such things, likes to see her husband's interest in another female's physical attributes.

Perhaps we may imagine an illustration of this fact. Let us say that a middle-aged woman is about to have a birthday. Her husband, who loves her dearly, plans a celebration of dinner and the theater for the occasion. She is delighted. Before the important day, she buys a new hat; she has her hair

done; she presses her dress; she makes sure she has fresh white
gloves, even weighs the matter of what kind of jewelry she
will wear. She dresses with the greatest care before leaving
for the city, taking endless pains with her make-up, all to
make herself look as pretty as possible for *him*. She goes off
in a flutter of anticipation, meets her husband at the expensive
restaurant he has chosen and follows the headwaiter to her
place, her cheeks flushed with excitement and her heart gay.
Then it happens. As soon as they are seated they see at the
next table a stunningly beautiful young blonde with a somewhat older man as her escort. The husband expels his breath
softly. "Do you see what I see?" he asks. "I'll have to give
the headwaiter an extra tip for *this* seat! Say, isn't she something to look at, though?"

The man is pleased. He adjusts his tie, sits a bit higher in
his chair, a certain indefinable zest having been added to the
meal for him. But for the wife it is as though a small chill
wind has blown across her happiness. All her preparations
for this great occasion seem suddenly futile. It is hard for her
to direct an animated conversation, especially as her husband's
glance keeps straying to the next table. She knows this
actually means nothing; she knows he loves her and her only;
yet, illogically or not, her bright pleasure in the evening has
been shadowed.

Now suppose the husband had been thoughtful not only in
providing a celebration for his wife's natal day, but in the
finer and deeper sense of keeping any normal reaction of his
from hurting her. Suppose as he noticed the beautiful blonde
he had said nothing, but turned to a consideration of the
menu. The wife would very probably have remarked some
time later, "Do you see that pretty girl over there?"

The husband would then take a long glance, as though noticing her for the first time. "She's good-looking, isn't she? Sort of the Hollywood type. Well, I'm like the French. I think a woman has to be a little older to have *real* charm," and his eyes would meet those of his wife.

Ah, then the heavens would open; the angels would sing! The evening would be pure bliss. And the odd thing is that any woman at any age, after such a speech, such a look from her husband, begins to be enveloped in a glowing beauty that comes only from a happy heart and a complete reassurance of love.

It is not always the man, however, who is responsible for such hurts as we have just mentioned. Some women, blessed by nature with certain qualities of charm and beauty, are likely always to attract masculine admiration and then, because they are flattered, to encourage it. This, for a married woman, is a grievous error. She may be as charming as she wishes and yet, by a subtle and indefinable attitude, let her admirer know that she has no interest in serious flirtation. She can be gay and lovely and yet manifestly untouchable. If wives in such circumstances use this technique (and every woman knows it) there will not be surprised, jealous and unhappy husbands' eyes watching from the periphery of the party circle.

In the long years of a normal marriage there are, as in life itself, many different stages, each demanding its own perfection of love. I would like to mention two which seem to me important. One in respect to the wife is that period in middle age when Nature releases her from the burden of childbearing but at the same time (due to what I heard one doctor term her only mistake!) plays havoc with the woman's nervous system. This is a time when the husband's tender thoughtfulness should rise to new heights of understanding. What the wife needs then is love and more love and constant verbal reassurance of it as well as perhaps a lightening of her household duties. The seriousness of this period's possible dangers was once brought home to me by a remark from our own family physician who has an extremely large practice. I asked him if he had found a certain rather new medication effective for women during this experience.

"Well," he said with the casualness which is often more shocking by its implication than something spoken profoundly, "I can say this. In the years I've been using this treatment I haven't had one woman *lose her mind*."

As the fifties melt into the sixties both husband and wife know that they are growing old. They may never refer to it, or they may make little jokes about it, but down inside they both feel it uncomfortably. Here it seems to me the woman has perhaps the advantage over the man. When her hair begins to turn gray she can if she wishes (and can afford it) have it "touched up" to keep its original color. But even if she decides to let the gray become grayer, she can have a different haircut that gives her an air of smartness. She can buy a hat which is a trifle daring; she can use new colors to give a suggestion of youth. She can do a dozen little things which, while they may deceive no one about her real age, do give her a psychological uplift and a more pleasing appearance.

But a man can do none of these things. When his hair begins to turn gray, all he can do is hope that it will not disappear altogether. He cannot raise his spirits by brightening his costume. Aside from a change of neckties he is forever condemned to a practically statutory sobriety and sameness of apparel. He must watch helplessly as time puts its mark upon him. And because he says nothing about it his wife may not realize how keenly he feels his sagging cheek muscles and the widening bald spot on top of his head. A cold hand seems to grip him as retirement looms ahead, setting its fixed boundary between the active work which has occupied most of his life and the untried leisure he is not sure he will enjoy. These are hard years for a husband, and the unselfishly thoughtful wife will look beneath his mask and give him comfort.

But there is something deeper which brings the fact of old age poignantly home to a man. He finds that he can be no longer the ardent lover of the past years. Physiological changes have robbed him of a power that was at once his pride and one great source of his joy in life. He may consequently have a feeling of frustration and the imminence of age.

Here again, wives, I think, are slow to realize the great unspoken need in the hearts of their husbands at this time. This need is for reassurance, for confidence. Every additional tenderness helps, but the need is also for emphasis upon his essential virility, spiritual if not physical.

Through the years the man is the titular head of the house. He is the wage earner and his greater physical strength has from the beginning of history afforded a protectiveness for his family. If he arbitrarily *dominates* his home, he falls from the perfection of love and becomes that unlovely thing, the "boss," instead of a devoted partner. So in all family councils the wife's opinions and wishes should be considered on a par with those of her husband. This is true partnership, this is a happy union. For though the man is the material provider, the woman *makes* the home; establishes its atmosphere, bears the children and is the giver in love of her own precious body.

There is, however, a very real and gracious deference that should always be accorded to him who sits at the head of the table; and at no time is this more essential than when the years begin to take their toll of a strong man's strength.

The context of the strange command which set me thinking along these lines deals with love in its widest sense: the love of the world. This is at once the most difficult of all the lessons of love and the least practiced. Yet there is a magnificent compulsion, a terrible urgency in these words of Jesus. God, he says, sends his rain upon the just and the unjust; he makes his sun to shine on the bad as well as the good, so we all must be as perfect as He in our love of our fellow men. This is startling, this is revolutionary, but oh, just could it be the key to the world's survival? Could love prove stronger than missiles in the long run? How could this be achieved? How will we ever know? Perhaps as there certainly are great untapped reservoirs of power in prayer, so there may be in love, poured out like a sacrifice by you and me and the man next to you and the woman who is my neighbor and so on and on. Someday when weapons of destruction fail, the world may try love — if it is not too late. Would that it could be now!

I feel the great inadequacy of this chapter. I may have seemed to cite foolish examples and, since I had to be selective, to put the emphasis on the least important things. I can only say this. I have written this with the deepest feeling out of my heart. I have been, I suppose, like most wives and mothers, a day-by-day unselfish person in my consuming interest in, and concern for my family. But as I look back over the years I see plainly now that from my young womanhood on, when confronted (as I was) with unusual problems and crises, I often failed to rise to that peak of perfection in love which I should have and *could* have reached, if I had not in certain ways thought of myself. So I have written these pages in the hope that someone reading them may catch a vision of that perfection of love through unselfishness which I believe is possible, and which may very likely be the only perfection attainable in this fallible world.

VI
The Duty of Happiness

"The merry heart doeth good like a medicine."

THE WHOLE QUESTION of duty has provided much ground for argument. Those of the older generations spelled it with a capital *D* and, unfortunately, made it synonymous with that which was hard and disagreeable. In our modern times there has been a revolt against this attitude. Those of the so-called New Freedom have been resentful of anything like moral obligation. Because the feeling persists, as a sort of Puritan inheritance, that any duty is unpleasant, they eschew the whole idea. I remember once in a conversation with a certain man who had great independence of spirit I mentioned that I felt such and such a thing to be a duty. His reaction was extreme.

"Duty!" he almost shouted, "I hate that word."

Words unfortunately collect through the years certain connotations which sometimes obscure part of their true meaning. I think this has happened to the word in question.

Coming upon it obliquely we find new light in the definition of *obligation* according to Webster's Unabridged: "Any duty imposed by law, promise or contract, by the relations of society, *or by courtesy, kindness, etc.*"

This last phrase at once lifts the conception of duty out of the completely burdensome. It suggests that a duty might possibly run parallel with our normal inclinations. We can think of many examples of this. The expression, "It now becomes my *pleasant* duty . . ." is heard often enough to convince us that duty and pleasure are not mutually incompatible. The duties connected with courtesy and kindness are generally delightful exercises. So it may not sound too bizarre if I state that I have come to believe that it is our *duty* to be happy.

I realize, however, that although this idea is not original with me it may need some explanation. With the dark theological shadow of the Puritan and the Calvinist still upon us, and the manifold anxieties of the present day weighing down the spirit, this may at first thought sound foolish and even flippant; but I wish to present my case.

In the first place we need to consider the meaning of happiness itself and its relation to the general order of the universe. It is, like all emotions, relative and capable of great difference in degree. It runs the gamut through felicity, beatitude and bliss itself. But for most of us the word denotes an excitation of pleasure and contentment, a conscious sense of well-being as opposed to the normal disruptive ills of life. It is recognized by all as a boon, as something immeasurably valuable, a consummation for which all mankind strives in pathetically eager ways. While there may be almost as many

imagined causes of it and as many lines of pursuit as there are
men and women, the object, the ultimate goal is always the
same. So the supreme importance of happiness goes unquestioned.

The poet Wilfred Blunt puts this latter idea very strongly
when he says:

> He who has once been happy is for aye
> Out of destruction's reach.

If happiness, however, is to be considered a duty it must be
related somehow to the general moral order, and this I think
can be done. First of all, there is evidence that happiness is
implicit in the universe even as suffering, and perhaps to a
greater degree. There is, for example, more beneficence and
fruition in nature than destruction; there is more natural
beauty of color, light and sound than there is ugliness; there
are the signs of natural, instinctive happiness in the songs of
birds, the playfulness of animals and the prevalence of *laughter* in mankind. This latter interests me greatly. It is at once
the commonest and the strangest of all man's reactions to life.
He has been described as the *risible* animal. He alone laughs in
the face of the universe. There is perhaps something deeper
here than we think in connection with this uniqueness.
Laughter comes only, the psychologists tell us, because of
recognition of a deviation from the normal. This awareness
may be quite unconscious, but it means that when a man
laughs he actually accepts the natural order of the universe
and is amused by whatever, even in the smallest degree, runs
counter to it. This reaction may show pure mirth or bravado
or courage, or, and this is by far the most important possibility, an unconscious inner conviction that "all will yet be

well." It just may be that the evidence of man's ultimate indestructibility lies not in his prayers alone, but in his laughter.

One great support to the validity of the thought of happiness as a moral concept is that it is a positive, dynamic force for good, while its opposites — the emotions of discontent, sorrow, remorse or despair — are now definitely known to be destructive not only to the mind, but to the actual tissue of the body itself. Psychosomatic disease is now soberly recognized; at the same time it has been proven that happiness, all other things being equal, induces health.

Happiness is then a beneficial thing; it is exhilarating, it is constructive, it increases human potential. (Ask any employer whether he likes to have *unhappy* men in his service!) It is a force, indeed, which seems to act in line with the divine plan. There is a sort of electric eagerness about the condition of happiness which generates activity. William James says: "Whenever a process of life communicates an eagerness to him who lives it, there the life becomes genuinely significant." So the happy person may be said to have a sort of cosmic significance.

Another quality of happiness which relates it to the moral order is that it is never solitary. It communicates itself to all within reach. There is a shining circle about a happy person which energizes and brightens all who come within it. In other words, the happiness of even one person radiates a positive and constructive force, lets loose a certain dynamic energy which may affect many people for good even as the little candle throws its light afar. It is conceivable then that the cultivation of a happy spirit and the full exercise of joy whenever possible may actually constitute a conformity to the laws of God.

But even if we should all agree to the concept of happiness as a *duty*, there are still large obstacles in the path of its pursuance. Not that we argue against the feeling itself. Far from it. As I have said, the whole human race pathetically craves it. The unfortunate fact is that so few people seem to have it steadily and consistently and *consciously* in their lives, as an elixir upon which they may depend. Perhaps we are all inclined to think of it rather as a sort of rainbow which comes occasionally and quickly disappears, a transient glory which colors our sky for a brief time and then leaves it a dull gray again.

There are all too valid reasons for this attitude. Our beautiful and wonderful world is not, as the old hymn puts it, "a flowery bed of ease." It is not Utopia. Sickness, pain, sorrow, anxiety and disappointment invade every life. There is, moreover, by a curious and unexplainable disposition of genes, a difference in human personality. Some people are by nature gay, easily optimistic, filled with a simple *joie de vivre*, while others through no fault of theirs are inclined toward somberness and pessimism. There are many impediments to the desired end which must be honestly faced. The question is, can we accept them as they enter our lives and still know general happiness?

In the first place I believe we should often force ourselves to remember that happiness is not an outward state but an inner condition. Even the very young soon learn the folly of assuming that the man in the community who has the biggest house, the greatest number of cars and the most money in the bank is the happiest one. Circumstances may prove he is of all men the most miserable. Happiness, therefore, is independent of externals and is a quality of mind and heart. This gives us the controlling key. If we were to be completely dependent for happiness upon the shifting winds of fortune we could scarcely think of it as a duty. We would then need to accept no responsibility in regard to it. But if it is caused primarily by our own inner attitudes then, indeed, we may not only have stronger hopes of possessing it, but we may clearly assume our obligation in regard to it.

One of the greatest living French writers is André Maurois. I read recently a book of his called *To an Unknown Lady*. Unlike most of his work this little volume has a light, almost playful touch but in it he manages to put a great deal of profound wisdom. At one point he quotes Descartes: "My principle has ever been to attempt to overcome myself rather than fortune, and to change my desires rather than the natural order."

M. Maurois follows this up by saying: "Within the natural order, I am the storm and the sunshine: first to myself and then to those around me." He goes on then to state his own philosophy of life which bears directly upon this general point.

> To love the good in people around me, and to avoid the wicked; to enjoy my good fortune and to bear my ill, and to remember to forget, that has been my optimism. It has helped me to live. May it help you, too.

These words have particular meaning for me because I have such a pleasant memory of M. Maurois himself. Some years ago when on a visit to this country he was to lecture in our town and I was to have the honor of introducing him. I invited him to dinner so that we might meet before we went

upon the platform, and he promptly accepted. That evening
I did not have very capable help in the kitchen, so at six
o'clock (with dinner set for a half-hour later) I was at the
stove checking all the things to be done in the interim. Suddenly I heard my husband and daughter greeting someone at
the front door. It sounded from the conversation and laughter as if the newcomer were an old acquaintance. Who could
it be at this hour? I went to the living room to find out.
There was M. Maurois, easy, smiling, friendly. He had arrived by train, found he was early but had come on up to the
house. I knew he was one of the really great writers of our
time and also a man of the utmost sophistication, but I forgot
all that, both then and later at the dinner table with the other
guests. His gracious ease of manner, his attitude of quick enjoyment, and the serenity of his countenance proclaimed him
first of all an essentially happy man — one who, in his own
words, had elected to create within himself the sunshine,
rather than the storm. In his book to which I have referred
he says that during the war one of his fellow officers twitted
him upon his constant optimism. "If you were to fall from
the top of a precipice you would be quite confident you were
going to find a soft mattress upon which to light," he said.
What a beautiful compliment! For while, as I have mentioned, the optimistic outlook comes more readily to some
people than to others, the sort ascribed to M. Maurois is
brought about also by steady cultivation.

Even though we admit that happiness is primarily an inner
condition — an attitude, if you will — the most necessary
question is how one may so view the outer experience of life
that this inner and most enviable state may be achieved.

My first suggestion would be to concentrate upon the small joys rather than upon the great ones. There seems to be a natural human tendency to place happiness in the future. This is, in a sense, shifting our responsibility in regard to it. We constantly say, "Oh, if I only had such a thing! If only thus and thus would happen, *then* I would be happy!" There could be no greater mistake. Unless we are happy in the present moment the chances are we will not be so in a future one. This does not mean that unusual joys when they come do not bring tremendous elation; but it does mean that unless we are in a more or less constantly happy state, the effect of large beneficences will soon fade, leaving us dependent again upon another distant hope.

But the little pleasures that daily living holds, these are the stuff by which happiness can be sustained if we only have the wit and the purpose to appreciate them. The Greeks were masters of this fine art of enjoying life. "Dear to us ever," says Homer, "is the banquet and the harp and the dance *and changes of raiment and the warm bath and love and sleep.*" The italics are mine.

Oh, the little daily joys! How precious, how satisfying they can be! The morning sunlight on the breakfast table, the smell of the air at dusk, the silly jokes, the good book, the open fire, the flowers, the sound of the clock ticking, the hour when the family come home! This latter was the high spot in my own day through the years when my family were with me. I believe a woman should be on hand when her children and her husband return from school and office, and this daily meeting, after the short absence, with all its eager exchange of news was one of the chiefest of the "little" joys of my life.

As I write this I look out upon a world of snow. The blizzard began only last evening but now the wind-blown drifts are piled high and the houses and trees are heavy with white. Gently, quietly, a stop has been put to normal traffic and much of the outer business of living. There is power as well as beauty in the snow. And yet, could there be anything in all the world more seemingly insignificant, inconsequential and unimportant than one snowflake? As I watch the steadily falling feathery shower it seems to give the perfect illustration of what I have been trying to say. If we add the sum of all the little pleasures of heart, mind and body, including with Homer "the changes of raiment, the warm bath and love and sleep," we will find, I think, that the sum of them will be sufficient to condition our minds to an attitude of daily happiness.

In the face of overwhelming sorrow, even when we may find our spirits at first too stunned to take in any great spiritual consolation, I believe the recognition of certain trifling pleasures may give us some support. At the risk of seeming undignified I make a personal confession which may perhaps be of help to someone. In the first weeks after the death of my husband I woke each morning feeling so shattered in heart and body that I felt I could not start that day. I finally developed a small technique. While dressing I riveted my mind upon — my morning coffee and the crossword puzzle which I worked during breakfast! These two foolish things, pleasant in their insignificant ways, both in anticipation and in actuality, helped me to hold steady during those first waking hours.

I shall mention one other little device which has often been an aid to me, both because it is in itself amusing and because, strangely, *it works*. When I have been very depressed for any one of a variety of reasons I have forced myself *to smile to myself!* Now it seems absurd that the slight physical difference between having the corners of one's mouth turn down and having them turn up should affect the attitude of the mind, but it actually does. If you sit smiling to yourself, even though you have consciously compelled the smile, a slight feeling of optimism begins to creep over you. Just try it and see!

Perhaps this funny little outward trick of the forced smile may lead us naturally to think of one great moral obligation in connection with what we may call the *practice* of happiness, and that is its effect upon other people. No one ever wrote more variously and delightfully upon all phases of happiness than Robert Louis Stevenson, even when he had least reason to do so. A few of his comments are these:

> There is an idea abroad among moral people that they should make their neighbors good. One person I have to make good: myself. But my duty to my neighbor is much more nearly expressed by saying that I have to make him happy — if I may.

> There is no duty we so much underrate as the duty of being happy. [You see, he believed this too!]

> By being happy we sow anonymous benefits upon the world, which remain unknown even to ourselves, or when they are disclosed surprise nobody so much as their benefactor. A happy man or woman is a better thing to find than a five pound note! He or she is a radiating focus of good will; and their entrance into a room is as though another candle had been lighted. We need not care whether they can prove the forty-seventh proposition; they do a better thing than that, they practically demonstrate the great Theorem of the Liveableness of Life.

Even if we did not concede the duty of happiness for our own sakes we would have to accept the obligation of being happy because of the good it might do to others. Two lines from an old hymn point up this truth. They speak of

> A heart at leisure from itself
> To soothe and sympathize.

If we forcefully rid ourselves of the dark thoughts and anxieties that of necessity beset us all at times, we have given our hearts the *leisure* essential for perceiving the needs of others and sharing our fortitude and good hope with them. A completely unhappy heart has no leisure from itself. It is wrapped in a selfish cocoon of woe.

There is a certain accessory to happiness which I think should be mentioned and that is *fun*. This differs from the various diversions and amusements which every normal person needs and which most people have in some forms. Fun has in it more of merriment, of frolicsome or playful action or speech. It is likely to be more personal in that it occurs more easily with two people than with twenty, and inside the family rather than at large gatherings.

I had the great good fortune to grow up in a fun-loving family. My father and mother were both of a naturally happy disposition. They smiled easily. Our home was always filled with laughter. We had all sorts of private jokes. My father, always a rhymester, made ridiculous couplets; we all loved a pun. My mother and sister were good mimics and there was plenty of "character" material in our little town to draw from. There were also, as in every small village, constant stories of real life (some of them occasionally rather ribald) which ran up and down the long main street in waves of mirth and were savored with zest within the family circle.

When I was married this fun did not cease. My husband was a born wit, and his *bons mots* enlivened our days. We had innumerable little secret expressions which we found highly amusing; we delighted in outrageous puns; our daughter developed a delicately devastating gift of mimicry which sent us into gales of laughter at the dinner table. We were frequently hilarious over very small things. I realize, however, that in some families these particular reactions are neither natural nor easy. There are some people who, like the old Scotchman, "joke wi' diffeeculty." Once again, I think this habit of merriment can be cultivated. It is such an innocent one and costs so little. Jonathan Swift, the great Dean of Dublin, once said, "There are not many things cheaper than supposing and laughing."

If you have been born with a gift for the frolicsome, enjoy it and be thankful; if you find yourself overserious, try in every small way possible to follow the constant admonition which the young people give each other: *Have fun!*

But now to return to some of the deeper reasons for unhappiness and the possible cure for them. There are, to be sure, the ills of the body. We are in a sense prisoners of the flesh, and our spirits are affected by it. A wise and realistic old doctor once remarked that there were no deathbed ecstasies when the disease was below the diaphragm! In the midst of even ordinary aches and pains it is hard to be buoyant. Here is an anonymous sentence I once came across which always amuses and helps me: "Sometimes the body sits on a stump and has to be told by the happy Spirit, March on, brave one!"

When physical ills are very great, then there must be recourse to the deep reservoirs of hope and patience and courage which we all have within us if we decide to draw upon them.

But the emotional causes of unhappiness are perhaps the greater, and by far the most common — those involving sorrow, remorse and bitter disappointment. In this connection I would quote again one phrase from M. Maurois' own recipe for optimism: "to remember to forget." This seems to me clearly a duty which we owe to ourselves and to those around us. If we persist in dragging with us all the bitterness of grief, regret and frustration, like a ball and chain, we are making ourselves prisoners of the past. If we *remember to forget* the bitterness at least, we have freed ourselves for useful and cheerful service with the advent of each new day. This does not in any way mean the forgetfulness of the callous heart which out of pure selfishness refuses to remember anything which might disturb it. Far from it. The memories of our beloved dead, for example, should be kept constantly alive; their names should be often upon our lips; we owe them this immortality here and now. We should honestly face our remorse also (which comes in small or large degree to all sensitive and honest people) and pray for courage to bear it, all the while lifting up our heads and refusing to be crushed by it or to make it a daily companion. For all those who have dark valleys of experience from which it seems hard to emerge, there is a wonderful paragraph from John Donne, the great preacher of three hundred and fifty years ago. Perhaps no one else has ever set forth with such vivid and minute exactness the deep emotional morasses of the human heart; and because he had himself known them, his glorious consolation is replete with hope for all of us.

> He [God] brought light out of darkness, not out of lesser light; he can bring thy summer out of winter, though thou have no spring; though in the ways of fortune or understanding or conscience, thou have been benighted till now, wintered and frozen, clouded and eclipsed, damped and benumbed, smothered and stupefied till now, now God comes to thee, not as in the dawning of the day, not as in the bud of the spring, but as the sun at noon.

There is another form of unhappiness which it is our duty to throw off, and that is what, for want of a better term, I shall call philosophic gloom. This feeling, I believe, is rarely confessed but subtly pervades the thinking of many highly intelligent people. The mystery of life, the riddle of the universe, all the great unanswerable questions in connection with human destiny, bring to some minds a cynical beclouding.

Two great friends born a year apart in the nineteenth century were William James, the philosopher, and Oliver Wendell Holmes, Jr., the jurist. In a letter to Holmes when they were both young men, James makes this statement:

> In the confession of ignorance is nothing which the mind can close upon and clutch — it's a vanishing negation; while the pretension of knowledge is full of positively, massively-felt contents.

These two men, both profound thinkers upon the meaning of life, were likewise both optimists. We should certainly expect it of Holmes since he was the son of his father. You may recall that the elder Holmes, who was a physician (as well as a humorist), put up a sign in his first office: SMALL FEVERS THANKFULLY RECEIVED. I'm sure there was plenty of fun in that family!

Justice Holmes in an essay sets forth his views upon the re-action of man to the mysterious universe.

> Why should we employ the energy that is furnished us by the cosmos to defy it and to shake our fist at the sky? It seems to me silly. That the universe has in it more than we understand, that the private soldiers have not been told the plan of cam-paign, or even that there is one — has no bearing on our conduct. We still shall fight — all of us because we want to live, some, at least, because we want to realize our spontaneity and prove our powers, for the joy of it, and we may leave to the unknown the supposed final evaluation of that which in any event has value for us. It is enough for us that the universe has produced us and has within it, as less than it, all that we believe and love.

In other words these two great philosophers (for Holmes was one, too) say, in effect, there is much that we cannot understand, but why dwell upon our ignorance? Why not rather accept what little we do know, positively and happily.

And so, in conclusion, I feel that the practice of happiness is a duty, that it is possible, and that in some strange way it is linked up with the moral order of the universe. In support of the latter proposition in particular, I would like to give two final quotations from writers of long ago. The first is by a very young man who was known as the Shepherd of Hermas, A.D. 142–157. "Put all sadness from thee," he says, "for it is the sister of doubt and anger. It is the most mischievous of all spirits and the worst to the servants of God."

The other, probably the most concise observation ever made upon the subject of happiness, was penned by an older man, the author of Ecclesiastes: "For man should remember that life is short and that God approves of joy."

VII
The Quest

"Thou shalt love the Lord thy God . . . with all thy mind."

IN ONE SMALL PARTICULAR I hold a kinship with St. Paul. He states that he was brought up "in the most straitest sect of our religion," in his case that of the Pharisees; I grew up in another most straitest sect which was Scotch-Irish Presbyterianism. Probably there has never been a religious group which more intensely carried their beliefs into every area of their lives than did these adherents. The iron of the martyrs who shed their covenanting blood upon the Scottish moors was still in their veins. Racially rugged of body, rigid in determination, convinced of the absolute and equal validity of the Bible and the Westminster Shorter Catechism, they were among the bravest and most effective of the early pioneers in this country, dealing with the primeval forest and the Indians with one hand, as it were, and with predestination and "the elect" with the other.

In the early days great numbers of them settled in western

Pennsylvania and their descendants still hold a noticeable dominance in that section. Scratch a native Pittsburgher deeply enough and you are likely to find Scottish blood, which is only another way of saying Presbyterian. In our own little village of five hundred souls, we had (may Heaven forgive us!) four churches. Three of these, of slightly various forms of Presbyterianism, stood in neighborly proximity on one street, while a small Methodist church clung timidly but tenaciously to a sloping hill on another. The fact that members were drawn from a large farming community encircling the town and that every human being in the village itself (except our one reputed atheist) attended divine services, meant that all the churches were well filled Sunday after Sunday.

Our home was just across the street from the main Presbyterian church which for a hundred years had stood there in solid red brick, neither Norman nor Gothic, certainly, yet possessing a noble and dignified exterior all its own. Within, there was a large upper sanctuary with a "gallery" at the back (later removed) where the choir sat. For some years during my childhood my mother played the small reed organ there and I was allowed to sit in that delightfully exalted spot where I spent many happy hours looking down upon the backs of the congregation and deciding which of the ladies' hats I would choose if I could.

Below the sanctuary on the street level was another large room — then most uneuphoniously called "the basement," where Sunday School, prayer meetings and young people's groups convened, and where church suppers and sociables were held. On either side of the entrance to this area were two small enclosures known as "the men's room" and "the ladies' room." This did not at all mean, however, what the words would signify today. A fairly spacious wooden structure with a dividing wall, standing on the edge of the graveyard, should have borne these contemporary titles. No, the two little rooms were for the convenience of the country people who in snowy or bitter winter weather had to come wrapped in layers of extra clothing of which they divested themselves when they reached the church. The ladies' room was also used by the mothers who had to remove wailing infants from the sanctuary to pacify or feed them below. In those days children attended church from baptismal time on, and both minister and congregation had to become accustomed to a descant of soft coos or strident cries during the sermon.

In those faraway days we were all given to what a wise man once called "religious dissipation." The services which I attended as a matter of course in my early youth were, to wit: Sunday School at ten A.M., morning church at eleven, Young People's meeting at six thirty P.M. and evening church at eight — these all on the Sabbath Day, as the older folks reverently termed it. In addition there was the regular Midweek Prayer Meeting on Wednesday night. More than "assisting" in the French sense at these services, I did so literally by teaching a Sunday School class and often playing the organ or singing in the choir.

But there was more than met the eye in all these many meetings for worship. In those days there were no automobiles, no movies, no radio, no television. The church, while being the soul and center of the religious life of the community, performed unconsciously another function: it had a social significance as well. For most people Sunday was the day toward which the whole week moved — the day when people living far out in the country could be sure of meeting their town friends and vice versa. If a young farmer with a spanking rig or a brand new cutter wished to take his best girl somewhere on a Sunday night, there was literally nowhere else to go but to church. This latter situation made for a gently romantic atmosphere in the place of worship. Eyes were keenly, if discreetly, turned to see how many young couples were in the rear pews, for the number of times a young man brought a girl to evening church was a fairly good barometer as to his ultimate intentions. This service, too, was the one in which the minister lapsed a little from the calm theology of the morning to inject a faintly revivalistic note into his vesper sermon. The presence of the strange young males in the rear pews inspired this fire which though mild still added warmth and novelty to the message.

There was also a thrilling emotional moment for the young people of the town when the evening service was over. Before the last amen had died upon the air the unattached young men had made a hasty descent of the stairs and stood, lined up in the dusk, at the sides of the outer door from whence each emerged as the lady of his choice appeared, "to see her home."

Another aspect of the way church touched our secular life was that we bought our best clothes with only it in mind. There *might* be other occasions, of course, where we could wear a new hat or dress but the church services were the only certain ones. I have an amusing story about myself which illustrates this. When I first came as a bride to live near New

York I went, all aflutter, to a Fifth Avenue emporium to buy
a new coat. The first one the salesgirl showed me was definitely *pour le sport*. I knew perfectly well what I should say
but the words that came rose unconsciously from my early
experience. "Not that kind, please," I said, "I want a coat to
wear to church." I can still see and hear that girl as she moved
back to the racks. Out of the corner of her mouth she repeated ironically to another saleswoman, "She wants one *to
wear to church!*"

In our own home, religion was the central fact of our lives.
According to the old Scottish custom of family worship, my
father read a chapter from the Bible and offered prayer every
morning and every night through the years until he was
physically unable to do so. He began at Genesis and read
through to Revelations, then started with Genesis again.
Owing to this, my sister and I acquired quite without effort
a very comprehensive knowledge of the Bible.

The Presbyterians were the strictest of the Sabbatarians in
those days, so in our home we never played or sang secular
music on Sunday, and the idea of baking a pie or a cake on
that day was so preposterous that it never entered our heads.
As I recall, my father even shaved Saturday night! But while
all this may sound uncomfortably severe in custom, I never
chafed under it. This was largely due to the happy disposition of both my father and my mother which softened the
hard outline, and also to the rich humor which constantly
pervaded our household. When as we knelt in prayer the
cat jumped up on my father's broad back and settled herself
in purring comfort there until he rose, we all found this
amusing. When one morning at worship my father's tongue

slipped on St. Paul's injunction to "Salute Prisca" and rendered it "Salute Prissy" instead, we all went into gales of laughter once we were back "in the world again," so to speak, for Prissy was an extremely odd woman who lived just down the street from us.

When for some reason the hour was late and we were all tired, my mother would always say, "Just read a short psalm tonight, Alex," and he would always comply, switching perhaps from a lengthy chapter of Deuteronomy which should have been the fare for that evening.

When I was twelve years old I memorized the 107 answers to the Westminster Shorter Catechism, a really tough assignment. By naming the trees in our front yard *justification*, *adoption* and *sanctification* respectively, I was able to keep these three most ticklish theological pronouncements separate and managed at last to recite the whole without mistake to the superintendent of our Sunday School, as appointed. For this I received a beautiful Bible from the Presbyterian Board of Education, one which, while now rebound, I still use. My other reward, from the family, was a delicate alabasterlike vase which my mother, with her infallible taste, selected from the vast miscellany of our General Store which dispensed everything from safety pins, corsets and coffee to sleighs and plows.

Though I still have the Bible and the vase safely treasured over the years, I fear that most of the Catechism is now forgotten — as indeed much of it should be.

I may have seemed so far, perhaps, to have described the religious life of my youth with a somewhat light touch but I hasten to add that its depth and devoutness were incalculable.

By precept and example I was taught that the life of the soul was more important than that of the body and that the so-called means of grace should take precedence over all else. Needless to say, there was utter belief in the verbal inspiration of the Scriptures and their literal interpretation.

My feelings when I look back upon those long-ago church services are tender to the point of longing. The winter Sundays had the charming outer accompaniment of the chime of the sleigh bells as the country people came in sleds or cutters, for we always seemed to have snow in those days; but my fondest memories are of the summer hours of worship. I have only to close my eyes to see again the old sanctuary on a warm Sunday morning, as the congregation sat in their regular family pews. There was no "dim, religious light" here. Instead, the golden sunshine poured through tall, opened windows. I can still hear my father's soft tenor and my mother's contralto as we all sang:

> "O day of rest and gladness,
> O day of joy and light,
> O balm of care and sadness,
> Most beautiful, most bright."

Outside there would come the faint sound of song from the other nearby churches, and the occasional whinny or stamping from the long row of horses tied to the hitching posts that ran along the side.

But perhaps the most beautiful memory to me is that of evening church, a service little known in our present day. The sunset would be dying beyond the creek, and the gentle dusk showing through the open windows. Soft chirpings of the crickets added an undertone to the prayers and the

hymns. Oh, those evening hymns! How I loved them then.
How I love them still!

> Softly now the light of day
> Fades upon my sight away.

Or:

> Sun of my soul, thou Saviour dear,
> It is not night if Thou be near.

Then, of course, there was "Abide with Me" and "Lead,
Kindly Light," "Now the Day Is Over" and that lovely one
known as "Tallis's Evening Hymn," dating from 1567, which
our congregation sang so often:

> All praise to Thee, my God, this night,
> For all the blessings of the light;
> Keep me, O keep me, King of kings,
> Beneath Thine own Almighty wings.
>
> O may my soul on Thee repose,
> And with sweet sleep mine eyelids close;
> Sleep that shall me more vigorous make
> To serve my God when I awake.

Many times of a summer evening, too, when the service
was over and we had crossed the street to our own front
porch we would sit there, watching as the last lights were
put out in the church, listening as the last footsteps died away,
and then we would sing, the four of us, harmonizing on the
old hymns in the summer air. Usually we ended with the
same one before we left the soft darkness, or perhaps a full
moon above the church, and went off to bed. I have heard it
so seldom since my youth, but in words and music I think it
(Henley) is one of the most beautiful ever written.

> Come unto Me when shadows darkly gather;
> When the sad heart is weary and oppressed,
> Seeking for comfort from your heavenly Father,
> Come unto Me and coming, be at rest.

It was from this background that I set off in my late teens for a teachers college, then called a normal school, in a small county-seat town not too far away. I was, I think, rather young for my age, deeply religious, and very serious about my studies, though when chance offered as fond of fun as any. There was nothing in this new life to run counter to all I had known. A distinctly devout atmosphere pervaded the school: daily chapel services, an active Y.M.C.A. and a Y.W.C.A. in addition to many other exercises of worship. Two incidents stand out to me as having a permanent effect upon my own religious thinking. One was a special meeting of the girls called one Sunday evening by the very remarkable woman, Jane E. Leonard, who was Preceptress of the school. We went along the wide hall to chapel, a group of perhaps two hundred girls, noisy, giggling, wondering what "Aunt Jane" was going to reprimand us for this time. We settled none too quietly in the long seats and then watched curiously as Miss Leonard rose and came slowly forward to the front of the platform and stood there looking down upon us. She was well past eighty then with those long years of experience behind her. She stood without speaking, only looking at us with a tender solicitude as though touched by our youth, and wondering what she could pass on to us from the viewpoint of her great age.

We grew more and more quiet, watching her, and waiting, until at last you could have heard a pin drop. Then she spoke.

Without preliminary she recited slowly and with feeling Whittier's "Eternal Goodness."

> "So in the maddening maze of things
> And tossed by storm and flood
> To one fixed trust my spirit clings:
> I *know* that God is good."

As I recall she said nothing after completing the poem, but dismissed us immediately. We returned to our rooms subdued, and I, for one, never forgot her sermon.

The other incident occurred in a classroom. The teacher, Edna Bianca Smith, the finest English teacher I ever had, suddenly paused and for reasons of her own looked off over our heads and in her clipped, distinct accents quoted: "Truth is a staff rejected."

The statement struck me then, without my fully understanding it. Later on I was to need it, and appreciate it.

The years at the normal school ended in cap, gown, diploma, a poem as my commencement speech, and the great desire to go on for further study of English before I began to teach it. It was decided that I should go to the University of Chicago.

It was at about this time that I received what I've always considered the greatest compliment ever given me. Long before, in my parents' youth, a young man had come to teach in a sort of summer academy on our village green, in order to help himself financially through college and the theological seminary. He made many warm friends there who from that time on followed his career with keen interest as he completed his training, went as a missionary to India and became so noted as a Christian educator there that he was finally knighted by King George V of England, becoming Sir James Ewing.

On one of his leaves to the States he came to visit in our town and I had the great pleasure and honor of talking with him. When I left the room he said to my mother, "I would like to have her for India." My mother honestly reported this to me, perhaps with a little pang of fear that I might be influenced by it. But in spite of my deep and humble appreciation of his words — and also in spite of my youthful and fleeting considerations of a missionary career such as were probably entertained by many other girls brought up as I was in the missionary-conscious atmosphere of our churches and homes in which we knew by name those who were serving in Africa or China or India, Korea or the Indian reservations in the West — I did not give this serious thought but went on with my own plans.

When I reached the great University it was as though I had stepped into a new world. Everything was like magic to me: the beauty of the buildings; the sound of the "Alma Mater" played each night at ten on the famous Alice Freeman Palmer chimes; the delicious, unbelievable stimulation of classes and of people. Perhaps most of this stimulus came from the women living in the same hall, varying in age from very young girls to women in their thirties and forties working for their doctorates, and all coming from different parts of the United States. The ordinary, everyday meals took on, for me, the excitement of adventure. I came to them almost breathlessly, for here at table every subject under the sun was discussed by keenly intelligent people. In any small way I could, I eagerly took part in these conversations, listening all the while to those so much wiser and more experienced than I.

The city itself, and what it offered, was also a new door opening to me. It was here I heard my first grand opera and saw my first great art museum; but naturally the University courses themselves provided the great food, those in writing being to me a joy beyond compare.

It was in the midst of all this happiness, which in me amounted to a sort of Renaissance exhilaration, that something strange and, for a short time at least, devastating happened to me. Since I was a "special" student, I was allowed to select my classes. I chose all the English I could get and French, in which I was interested. One semester I had a blank in my schedule which I could not fill with either of these subjects. As I went over the list of available courses which might fit in with those already arranged for, my eye was caught and held by one. It was called: *The Psychology of Religious Experience*. My interest was immediate. I had had just enough beginner's psychology to whet my appetite for more, and the application of this penetrative science to religion was in line with the predominating force in my life. I signed up at once for the course.

The teacher was Dr. Edward Scribner Ames, a quiet, kindly, immensely tolerant man with a brilliant, seeking mind. Long years later each time I sought for an adjective to describe him, the word *Christlike* always occurred to me. He had that kind of gentle fearlessness. The students were of all ages, and I think the men were in the majority. I know now that the course was strong fare even for the oldest and most experienced; for a young girl with my particular background it was potent indeed. We used Dr. Ames's own book as our text, and from the first session I found it and the discussions based upon it absorbingly interesting. We began with the study of primitive religions, and for a few weeks I was engrossed, objectively, with the new facts before me. And then suddenly there came a change. All at once, as from one day to the next, these facts began to have subjective significance to me. I found that because of them I could no longer believe all that I had believed before.

I think I might have struggled more with my doubts if there had been any polemic quality in the teaching. But there was not; quite the contrary. The atmosphere of the classroom was one of reverent earnestness. In my deep distress of mind I marveled how so suddenly, so quietly my thinking had changed. This that had happened to me had come as gently but as inexorably as daylight turns to dark, or darkness becomes day. This variant from the beliefs I had heretofore taken for granted with a sort of sublime assurance was now a part of me.

Looking back on this experience I still wonder why it did not occur to me to drop out of the class when I first became disturbed by the facts it presented; but I am a little proud of that far-off young girl because she did not do this. I think I felt then, as I certainly do now, that our religion if it is to be a vital and honest force in our lives must never *run away* from the search for truth. So I finished the course, meanwhile wrestling with my problem alone. I never spoke of it to anyone, because it all seemed too sacred and personal a matter to share; but I remember I kept thinking then, If I ever marry and have a son or a daughter who goes through this experience in college years, I will not be shocked or critical or condemnatory. I will understand. Oh, *how* I will understand!

After my marriage I found that my husband's thinking was much like my own. We never had a son, but our daughter's attitude was essentially an inquiring one. Though I'm sure she never suffered the throes that I did, I do know that when her mind was expanding during the college period we had many long talks as we sat on at the dining room table after dinner that would probably not have been possible if our own minds had not traveled the paths they had.

The distress which I have described did not last too long. There were two reasons for this: one was that I was young and completely in love with life; the other was that little by little I realized that the great central core of faith was still mine; what I had lost were certain man-made theological dicta. As the years have passed I have thought much of the command of Jesus: "Thou shalt love the Lord thy God with all thy heart, and with all thy soul, *and with all thy mind.*" It has seemed to me that of all his teachings the last phrase is the least observed. There are great sections of the Christian church which actually discourage their membership from thinking freely about religion as they would about any other subject. They are supposed to accept blindly what they are taught and to question nothing. But is this not in direct contradiction to Jesus' commandment and his own example? The sentence my English teacher had thrown out once to the class came back to me with vital meaning: "Truth is a staff rejected." In my own case I had lost a certain staff upon which

I had leaned, but as far as my mind could discover I had accepted new truth and was doing my best to stand upright under it.

I am most interested in those young people who, as they use their expanding minds, begin quite normally to consider seriously for the first time the meaning of life and with it, often, the whole matter of religion. If when they feel their first questions rising within them, they fail to face them, if they run away from them, scurrying to cover as it were, even though these questions remain always hidden in the depths of their consciousness, this seems to me unfortunate. A man of integrity will not tell a lie to his fellow man. It seems worse to pretend to God that we believe certain things when we actually do not. But if you as a young person honestly and courageously face the doubts and problems that have risen in your mind, there is the other danger that because you find you must relinquish certain beliefs, you fear you have lost everything, that you no longer have a sure foundation. I wish I could tell you from my own experience that nothing could be farther from the truth.

In the first place, wherever your thinking may have led you, you will find you still have *God!* William James, my favorite philosopher, has a wonderful passage on this.

> How my mind and will which are not God, can yet cognize and leap to meet him, how I ever came to be so separate from him, and how God himself came to be at all, are problems that for the Theist can remain unsolved and unsoluble forever. It is sufficient for him to know that he simply is and needs God; and that behind this universe God simply is and will be forever, and will in some way hear his call.

And another greater than James once wrote:

> Lord, thou hast been our dwelling place in all generations. Before the mountains were brought forth, or ever thou hadst formed the earth and the world, even from everlasting to everlasting, thou art God.

You will still have the Master, himself, his example and his teachings — the Son of Man, as he loved to call himself. Try to see him with reality, not through a cloud of theological mists, but clearly, simply as he walked through the towns, by the lake, by the seaside of Galilee. See him as a young prophet with a great message, not of himself but of the *Father*, of the Kingdom, of life abundant; watch him go to his death for the truth he would not cease speaking, adjudged a heretic by the religionists of his own day; watch him until nothing else matters but the beauty of his soul, until you realize that you need fear the loss of nothing in your religion except *his spirit*, and that all truth is gain since he himself led the way to it.

You will have also that great book of the soul's pilgrimage which we call the Bible. One of your difficulties may be that you suddenly find you cannot believe everything in it literally. But you still have the great mass of spiritual truth which is the important part. Jesus himself said: ". . . the letter killeth, but the spirit giveth life."

You have prayer, that mysterious link between man and God, the validity of which you can prove for yourself; and you have also, if you will only avail yourself of them, the great comforting, soul-nourishing services of the church.

Above all, I would say to those of you young people who have experienced doubts, do not be ashamed of them. God has ordained that there shall always be in the world two essentially different types of minds. The one looks backward, feeds upon established order, and preserves the sanctities of the past. The other is a seeking, inquiring one, respecting above everything else its own integrity; following its own leadings unfalteringly, even though they bring pain, if by so doing it may be utterly honest with itself. Both types of mind are noble and necessary. The first gives the world poise and balance; the second gives it progress and truth.

But it is not only to youth that certain doubts come with arresting and disturbing force. Older people also feel some-times, perhaps because of a catastrophe in their lives, that long-accepted beliefs have for some reason become open to ques-tion, and in consequence their hearts are troubled. Just re-cently in a book of devotional readings I came upon a frag-ment of a sermon preached by Rev. Frederick W. Robertson in 1861. I know no more of him than that, but this passage struck me as so tender, so understanding and so practical for all those in this particular kind of distress that I want to quote it.

> But there are hours, and they come to us all at some period of life or other, when the hand of Mystery seems to be heavy on the soul — when some life-shock scatters existence, leaves it a blank and dreary waste henceforth forever and there appears nothing of hope in all the expanse that stretches out. . . . Then the man whose faith rested on outward authority and not on inward life will find it give way: the authority of the priest: the authority of the church: or merely the authority of a document proved by miracles and backed by prophecy: the soul-conscious life here-after — God — will be an awful, desolate *Perhaps*. Well! In such moments you doubt all, whether Christianity be true:

whether Christ was man or God or a beautiful fable. You ask
bitterly like Pontius Pilate, What is Truth? In such an hour
what remains? I reply, Obedience. Leave those thoughts for the
present. Act — be merciful and gentle — honest: force yourself to abound in little services: try to do good to others: be true
to the Duty that you know. *That* must be right whatever else is
uncertain. And by all the laws of the human heart, by the word
of God, you shall not be left in doubt. Do that much of the
will of God which is plain to you, and you shall know of the
doctrine, whether it be of God.

And so, to sum it up, it seems to me that all that vast multi-
tude of devout people who have never known anything in
their religious lives except unquestioning and confident belief are, in their own way, blessed. But I feel that that other
great silent company, to whom I myself belong, are also
blessed in a different way. They have accepted the responsibilities of complete freedom of thought and, strangely,
through this, have become removed from fear.

I have long had the habit of going out from the house before bedtime to look up into the night sky at the beauty and
mystery of the starry firmament. At such times I have often
pondered on these thoughts I have just set down. And I have
been glad that humbly and honestly I have tried through the
years to love the Lord my God *with my mind*.

VIII
And At the Last

"O Morning Land!"

THE VILLAGE of my childhood, to which I have referred in these chapters, lay in a sort of quiet reticence among the Western Pennsylvania hills. It was very small, but self-sufficient and conscious of age and of worth. For this reason, probably, the farmer and artisan families who made up the community did not lightly take newcomers to themselves. As I look back now I marvel at the few changes in the town's populace outside of the normally recurring ones of birth and death. If a new family did occasionally move into the village, it never seemed to stay long. Perhaps its members subtly felt that they would never really belong there since their grandfathers had not also walked the uneven stones of the pavements or driven a team down the dusty course of the long main street.

With transients who came for a night's sojourn at the old stone hotel — which had housed travelers during a century

— or for a week's boarding there or elsewhere, it was different. These strangers could be enjoyed without reservation, discussed at night in the barber shop or by day in the
kitchen, conjectured about to the ultimate detail over supper
tables or around grate fires, without any of the responsibility
of permanent acceptance. They were beings apart, sent to
break the even course of the days. As they had come, so
would they go.

One spring, in April, a Young Lady from the city came to
board at the Miss Raineys' just up the street from us. There
were three Miss Raineys, all spinsters. They had left their
farm some years before and built a large square frame house
in town into which they moved with what I now know were
priceless antiques: a great clock which punctually told the
phases of the moon as well as the passing hours, quaint
wooden rockers, cherry tables and maple four-posters, old
teapots over which collectors would have gone mad. Because
their house was large and they were active, they occasionally
took a boarder.

The Young Lady had been ill, so the report went, and had
come out to our little village to rest and get some color in her
cheeks. Close upon this information came the news that she
was engaged to be married and received a letter from her
young man *every day*. This established her at once in my
mind as an object of profound emotional interest. Each
morning as I went to school in the bright sunshine, I thought
of her, for I was ripe for vicarious romance and she provided
it. I cannot recall her face too clearly except that it was
beautiful and kind. Her hair was chestnut brown and worn
in heavy braids around her head. She kept to the house for

the most part, but early each evening she walked down to the post office for her mail, and then repassed our house slowly, reading *the letter*. Once I saw her walking along our street with her heavy braids hanging down her back like those of a little girl. This touched me strangely.

One day at noon I ran to the drugstore to buy a chocolate pig. These were our most popular confections, satisfying enough in all conscience if they were found to contain only the sticky white filling that made up their interiors. But there was an element of chance involved in their purchase — a possibility of stupendous luck which set our youthful pulses beating wildly. Every once in so often as we bit carefully into a new pig's creamy vitals our teeth encountered a hard flat object. It was — a penny!

There were two schools of thought concerning the disposition of such winnings: The more conservative favored the hoarding of the penny for later use; the second and completely reckless advocated its immediate staking upon another pig. In either case our sporting instincts were aroused.

This day I had barely received the striped "poke" containing the pig when the druggist, who was also the postmaster, peered at me sharply over his glasses.

"You going right back to school?"

I was.

"You going past the Miss Raineys'?"

I was.

He hurried then to the other end of the store and brought forth from behind the glass tiers of mail cubicles a long pasteboard box.

"This come Special Delivery," he said, "and I haven't seen

anyone going that way till now. It's for the Young Lady
there. Careful now, with it!"

I forgot to bite the pig. I crammed the poke into my pina-
fore pocket. As I took the box into my arms I knew at once
by some special instinct that it contained flowers! And I even
knew the kind. I felt this before I had read the large sticker
in the corner.

It seemed incredible that I should be bearing roses to the
Young Lady from her lover. Roses in April! There were no
others in all the length and breadth of the town — perhaps
had never been before. Some blooming geraniums here and
there in a window, and in the garden beds the first pale
"Easter flowers," or a bluebottle, but never *roses* in April.
As I hurried on along the street the ordinary village sounds
became the music of the spheres.

I stumbled up the steps to the Miss Raineys' door and rang
the bell. The Young Lady herself answered it. I laid the box
in her arms, my cheeks hot with eagerness and embarrassment. I remember now how her face lighted and shone.

"Oh, *thank* you!" she said. And then again, "Oh, *thank*
you!" The happiness in her eyes blinded me.

This is really all that I saw of the Young Lady until that
last night at prayer meeting. Looking back now from the
standpoint of my own years and experience I am sure that I
know just the conversation that took place between her and
her young man before that last service. He had come out to
see her on a Wednesday afternoon and they would be sitting
in the Miss Raineys' big square sitting room. There would be
a bright fire in the grate because it was still early April; the
brass coal bucket would be burnished upon the black hearth;

the old clock in the corner would be ticking leisurely while the smiling moon at the top showed perhaps half his countenance; the rag carpet would be gay beneath their feet. There would come to them pleasantly the sounds from the kitchen as the three spinsters in freshly crimped hair and white aprons bustled about, preparing the supper, their thin, aging hands a bit tremulous as they though of the Young Man and his love, under their very roof!

I know now, as I say, what that conversation in the sitting room must have been.

She would speak first, looking up at him with those clear eyes. "Dear, I've such a *big* favor to ask of you. Such a queer, altogether absurd thing you'll think it!"

Of course he would not even be able to reply at once in words. When he could speak he would say, "Darling! As if there was anything under heaven I wouldn't do for you! I couldn't refuse you, no matter *what*. Tell me! I'll promise before I hear."

"Be careful. It's nothing you could imagine and you *will* laugh! But, you know I love this funny little town."

"I know."

"They're such *good* people. They even have a little church service on Wednesday nights. 'Midweek Prayer Meeting,' they call it, and . . ."

He would break in then, smiling.

"I see. You want me to go with you to prayer meeting! Not exactly my idea of the way we'd spend the evening but if you wish it, I'll go. Now, never, never doubt my love for you after this!"

But she would still be serious. She would twist his watch

chain slowly with her finger. Her lovely eyes would now be downcast.

"It's worse than that. I want us to *sing* for them at prayer meeting."

He would throw back his head then and laugh uproariously.

"Now I *know* it's a joke! Darling, this is really preposterous. You can't possibly mean it!"

"But I do. You see I've gone to these little meetings and sat there so quiet and peaceful and prayed . . . for us. And I've grown so much stronger. I'm going to be well, I'm sure, and I feel I *owe* something. I'd like to give something . . . from us."

He would not laugh then. He would look down at her and his own eyes would be wet.

"What could we sing?"

"Just some simple thing. . . . I brought a little music along, in case there was an instrument here. I'll find something. Oh, I *knew* you would!"

That evening was one of April's own. The air was cool and delicately fresh. The myrtle and Johnny-jump-ups were in bloom in the churchyard. For sounds, there was the rushing ripple of the creek below its banks, and the twilight notes of the robins.

We went to prayer meeting as usual. For a moment after I entered and sat down next to my mother I did not see them. Then I caught my breath in astonishment. At the front, beside Miss Bessie who played the small wheezy reed organ, were the Young Lady and her Young Man!

I had not seen him before and now tremors of emotion ran

through me. He was tall and strongly built with dark hair and a small mustache. He seemed much too large for the chair on which he sat and shifted his long legs nervously. He leaned always a bit toward her, however, with his arm thrown protectingly around the back of her chair. She sat serenely, her face grave and kind, watching the small audience enter and take their places.

I can see it all plainly even now. The soberly dressed women, most of them with many marks of care upon them; the men, weary after a hard day's work in the fields or at their trades, all sitting humbly there, awaiting the presence of God; and all watching on this night, as I was, with surprise and pleased expectancy, the presence of the strangers in the choir.

It was not until after the minister had made his "remarks" that the pause came for which we were all waiting. No hymn was announced but Miss Bessie went forward to the organ.

The Young Lady and her Young Man rose and stood together, his eyes upon the music they held between them, hers looking off, over and beyond us. Then they sang. The voices, baritone and contralto, were rich and beautifully blent.

> "Someday, we say, and turn our eyes
> Toward the fair hills of Paradise;
> Someday, sometime, a sweet new rest
> Shall blossom flowerlike in each breast;
> Someday their hands shall clasp our hand,
> Just over in the Morning Land.
> O Morning Land!"

I suppose I must have heard the song since, and yet, I have no definite recollection of doing so. Can it be possible,

I have asked myself, that from that moving moment the words have been fixed indelibly in my mind? In any case they have kept recurring to me through the years.

I never saw her after that night. She went back to the city the following week.

Then came summer and our little village drowsed in the heat; sweet peas bloomed in the gardens, horses clopped up and down through the dust of Main Street and the harvest moon rose above the church steeple out of a scented dusk. Autumn passed, too, with locusts trolling in the maple trees and rich smells of burning leaves and the preserving of the kindly fruits of the earth filling the air. Then winter, with its bright coal fires within and its banking snow and jingling bells outside.

But the round of the year was finally completed. The late snows melted, the creek began to sing, the birds twittered again in the church belfry and the plowman's voice rang out from the gardens. One evening in late April as my mother poured the sassafras tea at the supper table she spoke suddenly.

"Oh, I heard a sad piece of news today. Miss Nancy Rainey stopped on her way to the store and told me that the Young Lady that boarded with them for a while last spring is dead."

"Is that so?" said my father.

"Yes. It's a pity. She was married just after she was here. You know her young man came out to see her. Don't you remember? They sang a song one night at prayer meeting."

I sat very still, my sassafras tea untasted. I was seeing her as she stood that night with her young man beside her, her lovely head raised, her eyes looking far away as she sang, "O Morning Land!"

This poignant little incident has remained in my mind ever since, and often to myself I have sung the words of the song. A deeper significance, however, has been connected with it as the years have passed: a question, a doubt. Is there beyond all uncertainty a *Morning Land?* Is there, beyond all peradventure, a life after this one?

When I first began to wonder about this, I was ashamed. I kept it to myself. I was also afraid. I felt like one who had innocently opened a door to see a precipice yawning below. All the rich imagery of church ritual, of Scripture, of hymnology built up what seemed an impregnable defense of the belief in immortality. As far as I could discern, all my friends were assured, all men of God were confident. But one thing struck me as strange. If when a member of a family died, the ones left behind believed utterly that he had gone to a "land of light and glory" where in a relatively few years they would join him in eternal bliss, why, *why* the anguish of the grief? There was the loneliness of separation, true, but this has always seemed insufficient to account for the extreme desolation of sorrow. So I gradually began to wonder whether many people did not try to hold tenaciously to the belief in an afterlife, while underneath they had the same dark questioning that I had.

Another evidence of this came to me, oddly enough, in many Easter sermons. There seemed always to be an effort upon the part of the preachers to *prove*, to assert almost with violence the doctrine of immortality. I did not like the psychology of this. We do not try vehemently to prove the rising of the sun; we do not assert vociferously that the earth is round.

Now, the simplest way for many people in considering any moral or religious question is to offer the dicta of the Bible as the final authority. Thus and thus is true because the Bible says so. I love the Bible more than I can say. I was nurtured upon it. It is still my guide and solace. But I do not believe we can use it as *proof*. Its supreme value lies in an entirely different direction, that of moral truth. So, in this, the last of these chapters, I should like, if it is not too presumptuous, to set down certain facts and suggestions which lie entirely *outside the field of religion* but which seem to me to point to the possibility of an afterlife, all the while admitting, as I believe many honest, intelligent people do to themselves, that none of us can be perfectly sure of the validity of this hope until we each make the last great adventure.

Under hypnosis the mind of a person may go back and back through years of experiences long forgotten by the conscious mind. This is called age regression. There seems to me to be a much better case to be made out for what we may call age *pro*gression. For man in some curious way seems to glimpse that which is to come when there is yet no slightest ground for believing the idea may ever have fulfillment. It is at that point a conjecture, a fancy, a dream. Yet when such lays hold upon the human mind in spite of its apparent incredibility, man, racially speaking, never lets it go until it is consummated.

For example, consider flying, and the conquest of the air. It is centuries since this conception was first entertained seriously in a human mind; but it persisted, it kept rising to the surface in generation after generation until it grew into the commonplace fact we know today. It will be so with the trips to the moon and the other planets. Incredible, fantastic, impossible, but ever since the first whisper of the idea of space travel occurred to man, its ultimate realization was assured.

I know that these examples and all the others one could cite in connection with like discoveries are not true parallels to the problem of immortality, but I believe they hold significance in this sense: the idea of man's existence after death has been held by practically every race from the cave men on. Humankind will not let go of it. So it does not seem to me unreasonable to think that this, too, may be a whisper, a prophecy, a presage of a fact.

George Santayana has a remarkable line in which he speaks of trusting "the soul's invincible surmise." Surely this surmise that life continues after death is the most invincible of all. I would select then as one of the possible proofs of immortality mankind's insistent expectation of it.

In the second place there is that strange, and to most of us, unsubstantial body of testimony from those who assert they have had some communication with spirits who are no longer of this world, or have even seen them. I confess I have always been profoundly sceptical of this and have said to myself, "Nonsense!" But the older I grow the more often I recall that famous remark of Oliver Cromwell's, "My brethren, by the bowels of Christ I beseech you, bethink you that you may be mistaken." This is no age for flatly denying anything. We may doubt but we must not gainsay absolutely. So perhaps here it is not amiss to take note of the phenomena

involved in this *professed* proof of the existence of life after
death.

The other day I picked up a little English magazine which
comes to the house called *The Country-man*, "A Quarterly
non-Party Review and Miscellany of Rural Life and Work
for the English-speaking World." It deals with such subjects as new methods of feeding calves, the care of bees, a
colony of serotine bats, the use of new oxyacetylene tools to
mend farm machinery, and so on. It is as practical and of the
earth earthy as any periodical could possibly be. Yet when I
picked up the recent issue and scanned the lead articles listed
on the cover, I saw that the first one was "Ghosts I Have
Known."

I read it at once. It proved to be a simple, charming, almost casual description of a number of ghosts that the writer,
a woman, had seen from childhood on in various old country
houses in England which her parents had bought and restored
as a hobby. I would like to quote from this matter-of-fact
little article.

> When we moved to a black-and-white Tudor residence I
> met Shiltie, a noble old collie whose mortal remains lay in a cob-
> nut grove at the top of the garden. His finely engraved tomb-
> stone bore the inscription, "Here lieth Shiltie — our dearly be-
> loved friend — a faithful companion — a perfect gentleman.
> Died May 11th, 1846. Aged 15 years." I used to see him oc-
> casionally in the summer twilight sitting sedately under the giant
> walnut tree that grew on the lawn between the grove and the
> house. *Our dogs stood in respectful awe of him, always making
> a slight detour with tails at half mast whenever they passed that
> tree.* [The italics are mine.]

She speaks of often seeing when a child an old groom in

breeches, boots and leggings, sitting on a low stone wall behind the well, smiling to himself as he rebound the stock of a
carter's whip. She says that with the innocence of youth she
took him in her stride, even chatting to him though he never
answered, and adding this: "*Our dogs approved of him, too,
for they always wagged their tails and sat quietly nearby.*"
    Her last paragraph tells of a ghost whom she always called
"Sir Thomas."

> The only town ghost I have known lived in the dining-room of
> the Queen Anne house in London where my father practiced
> as a doctor. He always sat in a hooded armchair we had taken
> with the house, staring morosely out of the window. He must
> have hated the door to be left open, for although it had been re-
> hung several times it always slammed shut unless a heavy weight
> held it back, and even then it kept vibrating in a way that ir-
> ritated the diners and also the maids who came in and out with
> trays. On the other hand he must have loved cats for both of ours
> spent their lives in that chair, purring loudly. *Poor old Bruno,
> our spaniel, could not be persuaded to go into the room at all.*
> [The italics are mine.]

    This article, given the place of honor in the magazine, is
followed by a poem entitled "Cutting the Hedge," and this in
turn by an article on mules. It was this apparently calm acceptance by the editors of "Ghosts I Have Known" as fact
which gave me pause; and I have a feeling that many British
readers would also accept it with small reservation.
    I was especially struck by the author's references to the be-
havior of the dogs, for I at once recalled something I read
somewhere long ago in support of a spirit world about us.
That author cited the fact that a dog for no attributable reason may suddenly wag his tail as if in recognition of some-

thing unseen by man. I remembered, too, that beautiful old play of David Belasco's called *The Return of Peter Grimm*. When Peter comes back to his old home to set right a wrong he had done in his lifetime, and cannot "get through" to his family, he says sadly, "Yet the dog knew me."

There is very widespread belief through all Great Britain in the reality of what we rather crudely call ghosts. Every old castle possesses one and this is not treated as an entertaining fancy but as a reality, accepted and testified to by many sane and sober people. In Ireland and the Highlands of Scotland the belief in the intermingling of the spirit and material worlds is deeply rooted.

Some years ago at our dinner table we were entertaining a man and his wife whose home was in London but who had both grown up in Scotland. In the course of the conversation I told what I thought was a most amusing story of a woman I know who insisted she had once seen a leprechaun. To my amazement I found that our guests of honor were not laughing. The man was very sober.

"She may have seen something unusual at that," he said.

Suddenly he turned us to a very serious discussion of contacts with the supranormal. For one thing, he said that when he was a boy of perhaps twelve he had gone up the stairs in his home one evening to find an old gentleman standing in the upper hall. He had gone hastily down to the library where his father sat with his paper, and described to him what he had seen.

"Ah yes," the father answered, "that would be your grandfather." And he had gone on reading.

Now if the man who told this story had been an ignorant

person, or a fanciful and flighty one, it would have been easy to dismiss it; but the fact is that he is a highly cultivated, strong-minded, practical man of affairs who has fought through a war and, far from being insular, has traveled over most of the world in connection with his business.

It is interesting, I think, to note that these few examples I have quoted have all been of British origin. It seems that this belief in the reality of what we may call supranormal appearances is more strongly held in the Old World than in the New. There is perhaps good reason for this. In Great Britain, for example, the weight of great age lies upon landscape and dwellings. It permeates everything. It is impossible there to forget the past. It clings, it holds. Perhaps out of it there rises more naturally that which has once belonged to it. Climate also may have an effect. The heavy mists and rains that wipe out sharp outlines and blur the forms of the living could also make it more possible for spirits to walk half concealed; or, to my mind much more likely, could cause frequent hallucinations which are taken for fact.

In the New World it is different. In pioneer days the labor of felling the virgin forests, of fighting the Indians to protect his home left a man no time to dwell upon anything but the obsessive facts of present existence. The women, too, with their interminable hardships were concerned only with the realities of the world around them. It is no wonder then that their descendants, too, have not been greatly concerned with the supernatural.

But more than this, there is the American climate. We are not only a new country which the past does not dominate, but we are a country drenched in sunshine. Even in our homes we are well lighted. We do not have dotted all over our landscape vasty castles and manors with endless wings and dim and winding passageways. It is my thought that under these conditions there does not develop that *percipience*, as those in psychic research call it, which would enable men and women here to see spirit forms even if they were present to see.

This does not at all mean that there have not been many reports over the years of supernatural appearances in this country. There have been, indeed; but I do not believe that people in general here take such reports with the same credence that might be evinced in England, Scotland or Ireland for instance.

There is one odd fact in connection with the matter of *communication* with a spirit world which is interesting to note: that is that what we know as Spiritualism had its origin not in England, as one might have supposed, but in America!

When modern Spiritualism really developed with its use of "mediums" and all the paraphernalia for intercourse with another world, the "spiritualistic" movement spread like wildfire. England became interested in 1852, the phenomena there and all over Europe at first taking the form of "table turning," and the movement of objects without apparent explanation. When the seances became more and more common, many scientists and those interested in psychic research checked the manifestations with the greatest care. They found many of them to be fraudulent. (In our own country, you may recall, Houdini gave a challenge, never I believe accepted by any medium, that he could duplicate any occurrence at any seance.) Before we, as ordinary matter-of-fact people dismiss the whole matter of spiritualism as imposture, however, we must take note again of the fact that some of the world's greatest scientists have taken the matter seriously enough to study it with profound care. In sorting out the elements of truth in all these proceedings they first testified to the authenticity of telepathy, a method by which mind seemed under certain conditions to communicate with mind without material media. This opened the way for at least thoughtful consideration of some of the stranger phenomena. In connection with this I felt that the most sober and factual report would be found in the latest edition of the *Encyclopaedia Britannica*, and so I wish to quote now from it.

> The discovery of telepathy, that is to say the transference of thought or of ideas or emotions from one person to another without the use of any of the normal means of communication — a power which has been established by direct experiment as possessed by some people — tends to throw light upon these apparitions and indeed upon the whole spiritistic hypothesis. For if it is possible for one mind to influence another without the use of the material mechanism commonly employed, it tends to demonstrate an independence between mind and body which cannot fail to have important implications. . . . Now mental activity apart from the body is of the essence of the spiritistic hypothesis: and there would be no reason to object to the idea that deceased people can communicate information provided the great and fundamental step is taken of assuming that they still continue to exist.

In summing up the statements concerning the more incredible phenomena induced by various mediums through ectoplasm, a substance which seems not of this world, which apparently emanates from the medium's body and returns to it, the author says:

In quoting such assertions it is not to be supposed that they are as yet fully accepted; but they indicate the lines on which investigation should proceed. The hypothesis gives a link on which the phenomena can be threaded together, so as to give them a sort of coherence which further experience may either substantiate or discard.

He further says that spiritualistic phenomena have been testified to by all nations and peoples, have been spread over all sorts of historical documents from the Old Testament on, have passed through a time of much scepticism and contumely "until they have emerged in the moderate and cautiously sceptical atmosphere of today."

As we consider again that some of the finest scientists of the last century have seriously studied the findings of spiritualism, perhaps we, too, should be *cautiously* sceptical.

One distinguished English scientist who much later carried on his own experiments with what we may call "interworld" communication was Sir Oliver Lodge whose testimony is partially contained in his poignant book, *Raymond,* published after the First World War in which his son was killed. It was said by some critics at the time, I remember, that the author's great grief had perhaps dulled his usual scientific method of approach; that his conviction that he had held communication with his son was the result of a highly charged emotional state. But I was never entirely convinced of this, for I heard Sir Oliver lecture in the twenties when he came to New York. His subject was "The Reality of the Unseen," and the impression of it and of him would still be strong in me after all the years even if I did not have the notes I took at that time.

I remember him as a large man, straightforward, modest, kindly in personality. He spoke in a strong, even voice, weighing each sentence carefully as a man accustomed to speaking only what he has learned at great cost and knows to be true. The first part of his lecture dealt with the reasons why we should count nothing impossible in the realm of the unseen since we have already accepted so much as fact. He spoke of the particles of the atom revolving around each other according to a law as certain and fixed as that which governs the planets; of the ethereal tremors, millions of millions in a second of time which produce light; he said finally that it is only the *unseen* things which are the permanent realities — that matter and space are real for a time but they are transient.

In connection with this he stated that the real, *permanent* self is not the brain; that the brain is merely a watery mass which serves to connect, or transmit between, the real self and the outer world. He said he was coming to believe that the so-called dead have bodies of ether and live just around us!

His conclusion was to me the most striking part of his whole lecture.

"I am now convinced," he stated, "that it is possible to have communication with those in the other world, but I am also convinced that this is something which the average person should *let alone*."

Those last words added, for me, validity to everything he had said before.

So, in regard to all this matter of the supernatural world impinging upon our own, most of us cannot easily believe, without reservation, the really voluminous testimony of those who feel they have seen and heard manifestations of a spiritual sort. But we should perhaps stop to realize that these experiences (as already noted) have happened in all ages and in all countries, that they have penetrated not only the folklore of the world but our finest literature, and that men of unquestioned scientific renown, some of whom are now working on this problem in American universities, have found that while many of these materializations have been either fraudulent or in the nature of hallucinations, there still remains a considerable body of phenomena which have either been proven or which cannot either be affirmed or denied.

I have sometimes thought of radio as an illustration of this possibility. Due to a delicately wrought and sensitized receiving apparatus the radio brings us sounds which are already in the air all around us but which we cannot of ourselves hear. This of course holds true in greater and even more miraculous degree of television. Could it be that certain people, possessed of a peculiar extrasensory perception, are attuned to a reception of sights and sounds that the average person is not? These would then justly be known (as the men in psychic research call them) as *percipients*, those who can receive supersensible impressions.

To sum up the second part of this chapter I feel that we should with open minds accept whatever residuum of evidence remains when the false and mistaken is removed from the testimony concerning the supranormal, and add its weight for whatever it is worth (and suggestively I think it *is* worth much) to the first point we discussed of man's insistent expectation of a life beyond this one. But, like Sir Oliver

Lodge, I believe that after this consideration and acceptance, any experimentation with it is a good thing for the average person to let alone.

But the third and by far the most important element of proof of a life beyond this comes to me from what at first thought seems the most unlikely source of all, and that is modern science. From the time when Charles Darwin put forth his remarkable findings in *The Origin of Species* down to the present day there have been some people who feel that science is the enemy of religion. This opinion is unfortunate. While in Mr. Darwin's day, and for years after, it was necessary for thoughtful people to make adjustments in their thinking, there has developed a gradual willingness to admit that scientific findings in connection with life in general may be correct. Truth is like daylight. You cannot prevent its coming. You cannot hold it back. Gently, inexorably it spreads. If you insist upon closing your eyes to it you have not changed its force nor its reality. In this age of man-made satellites, and of seriously contemplated trips to the moon, as well as of the radio and television, the presumption grows that science must be respected and its conclusions believed.

One point on which it seemed long ago that science nullified the hope of immortality was that spirit apparently was utterly dependent upon matter and would perish with it. The dissolution of the flesh was an insuperable stumbling block. And oh, this surely is the cause of our sharpest grief! The dear flesh which we have loved, which has been the precious vehicle of the personality. As we see death claim one of our own, it is the familiar *body* which we feel we cannot give up. Here is anguish upon anguish!

And yet, to those in sorrow, as time goes on, the body we mourn recedes a little and the spirit of the one gone gradually rises more strongly in the mind. It is at this point that modern science has brought me comfort. The belief in a *disembodied* consciousness is unthinkable, intolerable. Is there then something in the inexhaustible resources of this universe which we may hopefully believe affords a new body to replace the one of flesh? There is much in the new science to support this hope.

The scientists themselves now say that when they get down to the atoms and the electrons and so on, they have actually touched the borderland where matter and energy seem to merge into one another. It looks, indeed, as though the physicists and the psychologists have followed their quests along converging lines so that at their meeting point they find that matter and what we call spirit are practically the same. Each in its ultimate form may be either. As Sir William Crookes, a great English scientist, says: "I venture to think that the greatest scientific problems of the future will find their solution in this borderland and even beyond. Here it seems to me lie ultimate realities, subtle, far reaching, wonderful."

I would like to quote from a book called *Immortability*, written by the late Dr. S. D. McConnell. He says: "The observed interdependence of body and soul which has so weighed down the hope of immortality may prove the rescue of that hope."

He goes on further to say:

The truth would seem to be that we are beginning to take serious account of a set of unclassified psychic phenomena which correspond very closely with a newly described set of physical phenomena. The unthinking person is prone to regard such things as wireless telegraphy and Roentgen photography and radio transmission as merely inventions or discoveries which are only a little more wonderful in degree than the hundreds which precede them, but not differing from them in kind. This misapprehends their significance. They are discoveries in an entirely new region. They are doors opened into another universe. It is a material universe to be sure and one which we now see to have been about us always. It is a universe where ordinary laws of matter are inoperative, indeed, appear to be nonexistent, but of its reality no one any longer doubts.

It does not seem too strange a presumption then to suppose that there is distributed throughout this newly discovered universe which exists all around us a form of imperishable matter which may clothe the soul when its earthly vesture must be left behind. This is the comfort that comes to me from modern science, but which brings me right back, curiously enough, to that magnificent passage of St. Paul. Nineteen centuries ago he wrote with what seems now to us almost scientific precision (see Moffatt's Translation):

> Some will ask how do the dead rise? What kind of body do they have when they come? Foolish man: what you saw is not the body that is to be: it is a mere grain of wheat or some other grain. God gives it a body as he pleases, gives to each kind of seed a body of its own. There is an animate body. There is also a spiritual body. Thus, as we have borne the likeness of the material man so we are to bear the likeness of the heavenly man. For this perishing body must be invested with the imperishable, and this mortal body invested with immortality.

While, as I say, the discoveries of modern science have brought me this added proof of the soundness of the belief in an afterlife, I have honestly tried to face up to the alternative. Suppose it should not be within the gift of God to give us such a life; suppose his will is for the continuance of the race rather than of the individual, what then? Perhaps if we have known the warm glory of the sun and the white splendor of the moon; if we have felt the beauty of the world, and enjoyed friends and work and love, we should not feel cheated if we know nothing beyond. I remember a conversation I had some years ago concerning the death of an old clergyman who had been very dear to me. I was speaking with a brilliant young man who had also loved him, about the matter of immortality, and I have always remembered his final words about his old friend.

"He had life here," he said, "and he was such a gentleman he would not demand more of God."

Perhaps none of us should be demanding. For myself, if I knew now that the end for me would be to lie upon a certain quiet hillside near to the precious ones who gave me birth and next to him I have loved, I would feel I should still praise Him that at the last "He giveth his beloved sleep."

But oh, I hope, I *hope* and trust that the end will be but a beginning; that there will be in some sense a Morning Land; that in the words of old John Donne it will be "Good morrow to our waking souls!"